Graham Handley has taught and lectured for the past ~~~~~
years, and has examined at all levels from CSE to University Honours
Degree. After fifteen years in grammar schools, ten as Head of
Department, he was first Senior Lecturer then Principal Lecturer in
English at the College of All Saints, Tottenham. He was recently
Research Officer in English, Birkbeck College, University of London.
He lectures part-time for the University of London Department of
Extramural studies and teaches part-time at Enfield Chace Upper
School. He is the general editor of the Brodie's Notes series and has
written study guides in literature for Penguin, Macmillan and Basil
Blackwell.

Peter Wilkins is Head of English at the King's School, Ottery St
Mary.

Also available:

English coursework: **Drama and Poetry**

GCSE Brodie's Notes

English coursework
Prose

G. Handley MA PhD
P. Wilkins BA

Pan Books London and Sydney

First published 1987 by Pan Books Ltd
Cavaye Place, London SW10 9PG
9 8 7 6 5 4 3 2 1
© Pan Books 1987
ISBN 0 330 50258 1

Photoset by Rowland Phototypesetting Ltd
Bury St Edmunds, Suffolk
Printed and bound in Great Britain by
Richard Clay Ltd, Bungay, Suffolk

Contents

Acknowledgements

The authors and publishers wish to thank the following publishers, authors and agents for permission to reprint copyright material:

Victor Gollancz Ltd for an extract from *Z for Zachariah* by R. C. O'Brien; Laurence Pollinger Ltd and the Estate of Mrs Frieda Lawrence Ravagli for an extract from *Odour of Chrysanthemums* by D. H. Lawrence; Grafton Books, a Division of the Collins Publishing Group for an extract from *My Family and Other Animals* by Gerald Durrell; Secker and Warburg Ltd and the Estate of the Late Sonia Brownell Orwell for an extract from *Animal Farm* by George Orwell; William Heinemann Ltd for an extract from *To Kill a Mockingbird* by Harper Lee and for an extract from *Of Mice and Men* by John Steinbeck; Chatto and Windus for an extract from *Cider with Rosie* by Laurie Lee.

The authors also wish to thank the following for ideas and assistance in the preparation of this book: Kevin Dowling, Kenneth Hardacre and John Jenkins.

The GCSE examination

From 1988, there will be a single system of examining at 16 plus in England, Wales and Northern Ireland. The General Certificate of Secondary Education (GCSE) will replace the General Certificate of Education (GCE) and the Certificate of Secondary Education (CSE).

GCSE introduces several important changes in the way you are tested. First, the examinations will be structured so that you can show *what* you know rather than what you do *not* know. Of critical importance here is the work you produce during the course of the examination year which will be given much greater emphasis than before. Second, courses are set and marked by six examining groups instead of the previous twenty GCE/CSE boards. The groups are:

Northern Examining Association
Midland Examining Group
London and East Anglian Group
Southern Examining Group
Welsh Board
Northern Ireland Schools Examination Council

One of the most useful changes introduced by GCSE is the single award system of grades A–G. This should permit you and future employers to more accurately assess your qualifications.

GCSE	GCE 'O' Level	CSE
A	A	
B	B	
C	C	1
D	D	2
E	E	3
F	F	4
G		5

Remember that, whatever GCSE examinations you take, the grades you will be awarded will be based solely on how well you have done.

This book aims to help you by suggesting ways in which the coursework element may be approached. For detailed critical commentary on particular texts, we suggest you use the Brodie's Notes series (see p. 108).

Introduction

When this book is published many of you who read it will have done one year of your GCSE course, while the rest of you will be beginning the course which has two years to run. All of you will be concerned about your preparation of coursework. Your teachers will be guiding you and advising you in this preparation. None of you will yet have submitted a final file of coursework for assessment. This book sets out to guide you by indicating the range of the literature to which you are likely to be exposed; by outlining certain approaches to that literature; by providing questions, assignments, suggestions, notes, commentaries and ideas about some of the texts which you are likely to be studying. If you are not studying the named books, you will still find ideas and comments and approaches which may be easily adapted and applied to the books about which you are writing your coursework. Read the extracts, summaries and notes carefully. They will, we believe, help you towards a confident appraisal of what you read, give you a sound basis for your coursework, and point you in the direction of writing well. No one can write about literature for you. You must do that yourself, hopefully guided by your teacher and hopefully guided by what you read here. There is no short cut to the study of literature, to its interpretation, or to free writing arising from it. Self-discipline and imagination are the keys to unlock the enjoyment and satisfaction which comes from full understanding and appreciation of what you read.

Coursework

This book aims to help students who are taking English and English Literature in the GCSE examination by indicating how the compulsory coursework element of the examination may be approached. A number of extracts from books, and commentaries on books, are provided, together with questions and some guideline notes. All these are taken from prose books, the majority coming from novels, though some are from long or short stories, and some are from works of non-fiction. They may be used for either examination, although no single piece of work may be included in the coursework folders for both examinations. It will be apparent that a coursework folder for English – not English Literature – may also include writing such as stories, incidents, note-taking, summaries, letters, free composition not derived from any literature you may have studied. This book does not deal with those aspects of your course. Yet it must be emphasized here that the same reading material may be used both for coursework in English and in English Literature. The principle behind the selection of extracts and commentaries in this book is to give the student a model range which draws on established and contemporary literature. *Do not be put off by the fact that the particular books you are studying for coursework may not be included in extract form here. Study the treatment and approach to books and extracts, since this will provide the basic guide for you even though your material may be different. Read with discipline and imagination, think about what you read and write about it with the discipline and imagination you have brought to your reading.*

The term coursework quite simply means any work undertaken as a result of your studying certain texts. This allows for a very wide interpretation, and you will find as you work through this book that some of the questions and assignments follow traditional practice whereas others reflect current trends in the teaching and examination of literature. It should be stressed that no range of approaches can be entirely comprehensive, and that there are many and varied ways of reading and evaluating the huge body of work which would be generally agreed to constitute literature.

In English and English Literature continuous assessment of the student's work during the course accounts for anything from 20% to 100% of marks awarded, depending on the particular syllabus. Make sure that you know the precise wording of your examination syllabus, so that you are certain exactly how many pieces of coursework you will need to include in your final submission. You must know what variety they ought to be, of what length, and completed under what conditions.

The purpose of examination by means of coursework is to give you the opportunity to involve yourself more deeply in your work, so that you are not confined by time, or length of essay, or even by the efficiency of your memory. This new examination encourages the use of the texts being studied during the completion of the coursework assignments, just as plain texts or open book examinations have allowed candidates to take set books into the examination room. The student is expected to comment in detail on the part of the text in question, and is therefore not required to depend only on the recall of the outline or selected passages. Such a method of examination can be a great help to the dedicated and conscientious candidate, since it is calculated to reward genuine effort and appreciation. It gives you the time to read, think and write, and then if necessary to revise and re-write, and so produce what is your best work. Your approach to coursework is therefore vital: from the very beginning of the course it will show just how seriously you take the responsibility of entering for a public examination.

A unit of coursework is commonly expected to be about 400 words, or two sides of A4 paper approximately. Obviously a longer piece may be included from time to time, for example if you are carrying out an extensive investigation of an author, or looking at several works which are linked in some way. You will need to check with your teacher (and with the syllabus) to see exactly what you are allowed to do. The file you keep will be composed of the units you complete over the prescribed two years of the GCSE course. The best pieces will then be selected by your teacher and you for inclusion in the final examination folder.

In your coursework writing you should demonstrate the following qualities:

KNOWLEDGE   of what you have been reading, with a clear series of statements of what happens in the book or story, and what it is about.

UNDERSTANDING showing an awareness not only of the surface or literal meaning of the book or story but also of the deeper meaning that may be suggested or implied.

EVALUATION   reaching your own conclusions about what it is that makes the writing special (stimulating, inspiring, sad or moving, humorous or witty etc) and being able to express what it has meant to you.

The more thorough your knowledge of the books or stories (or extracts if for English and not for English Literature), the greater will be your understanding and consequently the more searching and genuine your evaluation and response is likely to be. There are no short cuts, there is no substitute for getting to know the texts really well. This means practising the discipline of reading and re-reading, thinking about them, discussing them with your friends; it means wherever possible reading what other writers have thought about them, and writing about them yourself. The questions, assignments and commentaries in the following chapters indicate ways in which you can develop and express the three important criteria listed above, namely KNOWLEDGE, UNDERSTANDING AND EVALUATION.

It will be of assistance to you to know what the examiner is likely to be looking for. Any assignment you are set may be designed to allow for responses at different levels. A basic answer to a question about the importance of the opening of Barry Hines's *Kes* might give some detail on the waking up of Jud and Billy before Jud has to go to the pit. A more perceptive answer would include reference to the language used, what the situation tells us about the characters, and it might also refer to the obvious poverty, the atmosphere, the potential violence and indeed the nature of the language used both by the author in description and the characters themselves. It might quote particularly telling phrases or words, and it might even indicate whether there is a moral comment in the presentation of the scene.

An indication of expected standards of achievement can be found in the GCSE grade descriptions in the syllabus booklet for the examination you are taking. Grades A B C are intended to measure broadly the standards covered by the former O level grades A B C and CSE grade 1; and grades D E F G to cover the standards measured by CSE grades 2, 3, 4 and 5. Generally for grades A/B on coursework involving literature you will be expected to demonstrate a high level of competence and to provide a full and complex treatment of the texts studied. Those which are prescribed for *close study* will need to be treated in detail with particular reference to content, style and theme. Candidates will have to undertake close analysis, supported by references and appropriate quotations where necessary. There should be an awareness of background, of the particular author in his time, of genre and of culture. The student should be able to recognize and identify features of the writer's use of language – imagery for example – and his or her sense of structure. He should be able to identify and discuss implicit as well as explicit meanings and attitudes within and across texts. This means being able to convey a sensitive, perceptive, imaginative and informed response, clearly argued, and perhaps with some evidence of originality. Personal as well as alternative interpretations should be sustained; valid conclusions could be drawn from comparisons made with other texts, or from wider reading. The good candidate will write with accuracy and control, in carefully organized paragraphs, with appropriate choice of vocabulary and construction of sentences. Very roughly, marks of 17–20 would record this level of attainment.

However, this indication must be regarded with a degree of caution, since the recommendations of the examining groups differ slightly. Teachers may well prefer to use letter grades, particularly in the early stages of the course before a final assessment has to be made. Marks or grades allocated during the course are *not* the final assessment. The coursework marked by one teacher or centre has to be moderated (compared and sometimes adjusted) together with coursework from other centres (schools or colleges) and then re-examined by senior moderators and examiners before a final decision is reached. This procedure is intended to reduce the element of subjectivity (personal judgement or preference with regard to content) in the initial marking, and to standardize the marks of candidates taught by different teachers in different centres.

For a C grade (marks 13–16 out of 20) you will generally need to be able to:

- write in paragraphs, using sentences of varying complexity, taking care with spelling and punctuation;

- present your material with clarity and accuracy;

- find relevant sections of the text to support your argument;

- give a general account of the text in your own words (for example, you would certainly need to be clear about the plot of a novel);

- give detailed references and quotations when required;

- show that you are aware of the theme or themes in the work;

- show that you understand the implications and attitudes in the writing;

- recognize and appreciate the way in which a writer uses language (imagery, description, dialogue, for example);

- show that you understand the characters and the way or ways in which they are presented;

- indicate the way a novel or story is structured;

- communicate to the reader of your work an informed personal response, that is, one based on knowledge and understanding and not merely the product of an instant superficial reaction.

At a lower level, for grades F/G (1–8 out of 20) candidates are generally expected to be able to:

- give an account of the book or story in a straightforward way, identifying points of interest in plot or theme. This would probably be limited to repetition of the story line or situation(s).

- show some knowledge/insight/perception of the books prescribed for detailed study;

- organize material coherently, for example in a reasonably correct sequence of paragraphs;

- recognize and be able to write a little about obvious aspects of style and ways of writing;

- communicate some personal response, with reasons for this;

- be able to describe the experience of reading the text, reflecting simply on what it has meant;

- make simple comparisons with other material studied, for example different texts by the same author, or on a similar theme perhaps;

- offer some reasoned judgement, for example on character and motive.

The range of work in your file is important. Most literature syllabuses require evidence of a wider reading beyond the prescribed texts. They also require some evidence of an ability to make sense of extracts from prose with which the student is not familiar. Examples of these should be available. The final examination coursework folder, as has been indicated, is a sample of the best work in your file; and since the file containing all of your work provides your entry to part or all of the examination, it is essential that that file is kept carefully. Date all pieces of work, keep a record sheet of the exact assignment, the time that was allowed for the preparation and completion of the assignment, the support that was available in terms of teaching, group discussion, background reading, film, video, broadcast, tape etc. What were the conditions under which it was finally written up? Was it at home, or in the library, using text and reference books as required, or was it in class, possibly under test conditions? The completeness of the presentation of the folder *will* count. Although we expect a piece of work to be judged for its quality and not according to the attractiveness of its presentation, it is unrealistic to imagine that legibility, accuracy and considered layout are not part of the process of communication. A good piece of work will be accurately written and neatly presented. Take a pride in your file, and make it show the tidiness of your mind as well as its quality.

By the time you have finished your course in GCSE English Literature, you should have a deeper understanding of the writer's craft. By examining a number of books of literary value, you will have been given stimulating insights into life and experiences. For instance, when you read an account of Gerald Durrell's early life on the Greek island of Corfu in his book *My Family and Other Animals* you enter the world of the author. You see the island in all its varied landscape with all its weird and fascinating characters. Gerald Durrell takes the reader through the cicada-haunted orchards and sunken gardens of the villas his family occupied. We see the olive groves, cyclamen woods, vineyards and cypress-shaded valleys of Corfu. 'The cobbled streets crammed with stalls that were piled high with gaily-coloured bales of cloth, mountains of shining sweetmeats, ornaments of beaten silver, fruit and vegetables.' Likewise, we may enter the world of Laurie Lee's childhood in the Cotswolds (*Cider with Rosie*) or the industrial Yorkshire of Barry Hines's *A Kestrel for a Knave*.

We may read novels like George Orwell's *1984* or *Animal Farm* conveying explicit political warnings about man's inhumanity to man, or Jack Shaefer's novel *Shane*, which reveals the way in which a young boy learns important lessons about life from the hero of the story. The themes and ideas which are a part of a novel will help to extend the range of *your* feelings and experiences.

The careful reading of a good book will show you the way to live more fully by giving more meaning to your relationships with other people. It is with human nature and relationships that literature is concerned, and this is what makes the study of it so rewarding.

GCSE English Literature syllabuses which have final examination papers

Board	Components	Comments on coursework (c/w)
LEAG	50% Paper (2hrs) Poetry and Prose 50% c/w (5 pieces)	Two on open reading of prose work e.g. novel, non-fiction, short story etc.
MEG	60% Paper (2¼hrs) 40% c/w (4–6 Units)	At least two assignments on open reading of prose work: novel, short story etc.
NEA	40% Paper (2hrs) 60% c/w (5 pieces)	At least one assignment on open reading of a prose work: novel, short story etc.
SEG	30% Paper 1 (1½hrs) 15% Paper 2 55% c/w (6 pieces)	At least two assignments on open reading (maybe one longer piece)
WJEC	50% Paper (2½hrs) 50% c/w (5 pieces)	At least two assignments on wider reading of prose fiction, short stories etc.

PLEASE NOTE many of the boards stipulate that *texts* studied for the final examination CANNOT be used for coursework, e.g. *Midland Examination Group*.

Open reading means the study, in less sustained detail, of a range of short stories, novels, non-fiction etc which will have been selected by your teacher from a list drawn up by the examination board.

GCSE English Literature syllabuses which have 100% coursework

Board	Components	Comments on coursework (c/w)
LEAG	10 Units	At least *two* assignments on a prose work: novel, short story etc.
MEG	10 Units	At least *one*, probably *two* assignments on prose work: novel, short story etc.
NEA	10 Pieces	(Only 5 to be submitted for final assessment.) At least *one* assignment on a prose work: novel, short story etc.
SEG	10 Pieces	At least *two* assignments on a prose work: novel, short story etc.

Fiction

You can expect to study a range of fiction for GCSE literature. Indeed, one of the drawbacks of the old examination system was that it offered too narrow a range of set texts. Under this system it was impossible to cater for the full range of abilities and interests. Obviously in the time available, your teacher will only be able to look closely at a limited number of texts. The books you study may well be established classics from English or American literature. They may be more recent novels which have achieved recognition in various ways, such as Stan Barstow's *Joby* or Ray Bradbury's *Farenheit 451*. Although much of the reading may occur in class, it is important for you to realize that there is no substitute for sustained reading in the privacy of your own home. It would be helpful, though not essential, if you possessed your own copy of the text. Here you are advised to get an edition which has been specially prepared and edited for school use; that is, it may contain questions and explanatory notes which will help you to a fuller appreciation of its qualities. Such notes and comments may prove particularly helpful if the novel or story concerned was written in a past century or even in the early part of the twentieth century. Sometimes words have a particular meaning for their own time, or the meaning has changed in our time. In any case, old-fashioned language may well need comment or explanation. You will also find that the Brodie's Notes literature guides which have been prepared by teachers and examiners on a wide range of prose – but more particularly on the novel – will be very helpful to you in interpreting, evaluating and enjoying the texts you are studying.

Approaching the novel

There can be no substitute for a close reading of the book you are studying. If you attempt to cut corners through skimpy reading, omitting difficult passages in the text, rushing, or inadequate attention to detail, you cannot hope to do well in this aspect of your coursework.

It is important for you to realize that there are many ways of reading appropriate to the required task. Wherever possible you should form some idea of the kind of coursework assignments you are expected to produce *before* you begin your reading. If, for example, you are expected to identify certain themes and ideas in the novel you are reading, have an awareness of this demand as your reading progresses. The idea is to *direct* your reading.

Your first objective in reading a novel is to form an idea of what it is about. This can best be done in the following way:

1 Read any summary of the novel often found on the back cover of the book – anything that may give you some information on the content of the story.

2 Skim through the novel and note its organization, its preface, chapter headings and any other information that is readily available.

When you read a book you should be putting into practise two reading techniques: skimming and scanning.

Skimming involves reading quickly to form a general impression of content. Think of a TV camera swiftly and smoothly covering a wide scene. Skimming is difficult to start with but is something which, like many good study skills, can be practised until it becomes a habit. To help you to develop this important reading skill you should practise these techniques:

1 Try to develop the habit of taking in groups of words rather than single words. Build this up slowly. Try two words at a time, then three words etc.

2 Look for the most important sentence in a paragraph. This is often the first sentence. You can sometimes form a good impression of the content of a chapter simply by reading the first sentence in each paragraph, but this is *not* intended to take the place of a detailed reading.

3 Seek opportunities to practise these techniques regularly when reading newspaper and magazine articles etc.

Skimming is important *when you have already completed* a thorough first reading of the novel. It may assist you in the search for relevant information to illustrate your answer or lend force to your argument. Skimming through parts of the novel may also help you when you are considering assignments of a more general nature, such as the development of plot and theme.

Scanning is an important technique to use when reading for detail. Think of a TV camera focusing on a particular subject, for example a face in a crowd. To develop this reading skill you should practise these techniques:

1 Look for key words in sentences and paragraphs. These will often give you the detail you need.

2 Practise scanning a particular paragraph quickly to try to spot the detail you are looking for. You may be able to develop this skill until you can scan a whole page to find the detail you require.

Scanning is particularly useful when you are being asked to identify points about characters, setting and language.

Reading the novel

When you make your first 'extensive' reading of the novel try to observe some of the following points:

1 Read the novel as thoroughly as you can. Try to discover any point of view the author may have, make notes on the setting, the characters, situations and incidents, and any significant difficulties in the plot.

2 Read the novel chapter by chapter. If you are forced to interrupt your reading half way through a chapter, skim over the first half before you return to a detailed reading of the remainder.

3 After you have read each chapter, try to see what purpose it fulfils in the novel. Should this prove difficult skim through the chapter again.

Preparation for coursework assignments

Planning

A professional writer would always give considerable thought to planning what he or she is going to say and to working out the sequence in which it will be said. You must follow the same practice with discipline and care. It usually happens that ideas will come into your mind in a very haphazard way as you first begin to think about the topic. You will find it useful, therefore, to write down all your ideas in note form as they occur to you. Once you have written down all your ideas in this way, then you can begin to assemble them into a more logical order. This will give you the material for each paragraph in your sequence.

Example

In Jane Austen's novel *Pride and Prejudice* Elizabeth Bennet is brought into contact with Mr Collins, Wickham and Darcy. They could be viewed as potential husbands. List the advantages and disadvantages of each from Elizabeth's point of view.

Take a blank piece of paper and write a brief summary of the characteristics of each of the men in the example given above. Look closely at the text to see that you are not just working from memory but are being accurate in your reproductions from the novel. You might even prefer to do this in the form of a diagram, with the advantages perhaps indicated as follows:

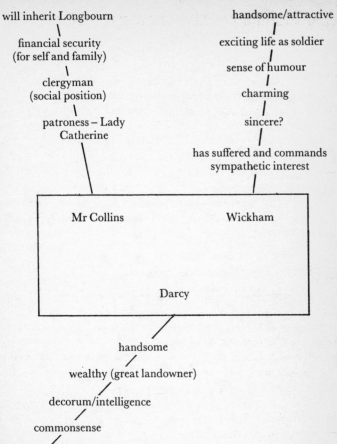

will inherit Longbourn

financial security
(for self and family)

clergyman
(social position)

patroness – Lady
Catherine

handsome/attractive

exciting life as soldier

sense of humour

charming

sincere?

has suffered and commands
sympathetic interest

Mr Collins   Wickham

Darcy

handsome

wealthy (great landowner)

decorum/intelligence

commonsense

kindness is revealed

Now draw a similar diagram listing the *disadvantages* from Elizabeth's point of view. You should have at the back of your mind Elizabeth's own character – her spirit, her wit, her particular 'pride' and, in relation to each of the men, her particular 'prejudice'. When you have completed your notes, the plan of your assignment might look something like this:

Introduction   Brief account of Elizabeth's relationship with Mr Collins (his proposal, the prelude to it etc). Her conversation(s) with Wickham and conversation/appraisal of Darcy. (Brief quotes if necessary.)

Para 2   *Mr Collins* – his advantages – the Longbourn inheritance – social position at Hunsford – patronage of Lady Catherine – security for Elizabeth and rest of family on Mr Bennet's death. A clergyman.

Para 3   Disadvantages – not attractive – pompous and dull – self-important and overbearing – obsequious – insensitive – humourless – snobbish – ill-bred. (Quotes.)

Para 4   *Wickham* – handsome – attractive – romantic – exciting life as soldier – initially invites sympathy – badly treated? – charming – apparently sincere and concerned.

Para 5   Disadvantages – little money or social position – unsteadiness of character – lies or distortions? – superficial – an opportunist – little real worth.

Para 6   *Darcy* – money and social position – intelligent – possessed of deep feelings (proposal to Elizabeth at Rosings) – kind, sincere (witness treatment of the Gardiners and efforts on behalf of Lydia) – handsome – attractive – commonsense.

Para 7   Disadvantages – proud – haughty – prejudiced – capable of error in judgement – appears a snob (the ball at Netherfield) – not lively.

Conclusion   Make clear that in the case of Mr Collins he only wants to marry (hence Charlotte) – Wickham is irresponsible and treacherous – Darcy reveals himself for what he really is by his devoted service to Elizabeth and her family. In the case of Wickham and Darcy Elizabeth's own feelings have been educated – she has developed and changed her attitudes in the light of what has happened.

The notes above are full, but of course, depending on the length of your assignment, you may not be able to get all the points listed above into your answer. Make sure you get the most important ones in.

Further assignments

Pride and Prejudice is a classic of our literature, and it lends itself readily to a whole range of assignments. You might consider some of the following:

1 Compare and contrast the various sisters in the Bennet family. Which of the girls do you prefer and why?

2 Consider the humour present in the characters of Mrs Bennet, Mr Collins and Lady Catherine de Bourgh. Give an account of a scene in which each of them appears (i.e. three scenes in all) bringing out the quality of the humour.

3 What do you consider the most dramatic incident in the novel? Describe what happens in it, and how it affects the plot of *Pride and Prejudice*.

4 Write a description of any social occasion in the novel, indicating the parts played by the various characters.

5 There are some important letters in *Pride and Prejudice*. Take any two of these – say one by Mr Collins and the one written in self-explanation by Darcy to Elizabeth – and say what they reveal of the characters and how they influence the events in the novel.

6 Imagine that you are Mrs Bennet. Write a letter from her to an old friend expressing her delight in the fact that she has three daughters married – Lydia, Jane, Elizabeth. You should try to capture some of Mrs Bennet's speech mannerisms (she will write in the same style as she speaks). Be sure to mention (a) her pride in Lydia's match (the match in effect where there can be the least pride); (b) her comments on the Jane–Bingley coming together; (c) her resentment of Darcy and finally her awe of him; (d) the fact that she is rather disappointed with Mr Bennet's responses generally – but then her friend will understand something of what Mr Bennet is like; (e) her expressions of triumph over Sir William Lucas; (f) some crowing over the putting down of Lady Catherine de Bourgh, but also some snobbery in the visit of Lady Catherine and the connection with her; (g) some expressions of delight in the MONEY her two daughters have married and (h) finally, perhaps, her hopes for Kitty and Mary. These are outline notes – introduce anything into your letter which typifies Mrs Bennet's attitude and behaviour in the novel, and refer to incidents in the novel to support your views.

Conclusion

1 When approaching the novel you should remember to use appropriate reading skills.

2 Make effective notes related to the *purpose* of your reading.

3 Assignments should be very carefully planned, as noted above.

4 Summarize and interpret, bearing the text of the novel constantly in mind. Quote in support of what you say, or refer to incidents, situations, character behaviour in the novel to help you make your point.

5 Be prepared to:
(a) write about the main aspects of the novel or part of the novel and
(b) write imaginatively about anything which arises from the novel which demonstrates that you have successfully absorbed any one (or more) of its theme(s), character(s), techniques, situations or style.

Plot

The plot of a novel is concerned with the way in which a story unravels itself. Contained within the story or narrative are incidents and episodes which are important to the development and resolution of the conflict or struggle which generally develops in the novel. The main idea here is for you to remember that you must know what happens in any story if you are to do yourself justice in an assignment.

Points to remember

1 Make *notes* during your reading and pay particular attention to the basic stages or steps in the plot from the beginning through to the end.

2 Make sure you understand the action of the story, listing anything of importance in it.

3 Make notes on each character as he or she appears. Try to see his or her place within the story.

4 Ask yourself what motivates the characters.

5 Try to visualize each new setting and make notes on the location described (see the section on *Setting* p. 41).

6 If relationships are particularly involved it may help you to construct a family tree. This might be particularly useful if you were reading Laurie Lee's *Cider With Rosie* or Emily Brontë's *Wuthering Heights*.

Most pieces of coursework will link themselves to specific areas of the book and to particular events. It is therefore essential for you to have made a list of what you consider to be significant episodes of the novel.

Here is a major incident contained in the plot of Harper Lee's novel *To Kill a Mockingbird*. Atticus Finch, a small town lawyer, living in one of the Southern United States of the 1930's, has taken upon himself the task of defending a negro, Tom Robinson, against the charge of raping a young white woman. At one point during the story it looks as if Tom is about to be lynched by an angry mob, and Atticus has to take immediate steps to prevent this. Atticus's problems are further increased by the sudden appearance of his children Scout and Jem, and their friend Dill. Although Atticus is at first embarrassed by their arrival and fearful for their safety, their appearance defuses a potentially tragic situation. At the end of the incident the children become more aware of their father's courage and determination, and Atticus is left feeling grateful and proud of the way the children have conducted themselves. The following piece of coursework is based on this incident.

Assignment

'You never really understand a person until you consider things from his point of view — until you climb into his skin and walk around in it.' Writing from Atticus's point of view, describe his feelings as he reflects upon the events which happen outside the jailhouse in Maycomb.

(Chapter 15)

You should skim through Chapter 15 of the novel to refresh your memory and to gain an overview of the more significant events. Firstly, note down the stages by which the story unravels itself. Secondly, a more *detailed* reading will provide you with enough information to 'flesh out' your assignment.

Stage 1
A rough summary of the events might look like this:
1 Atticus is told that a mob may try to kill Tom Robinson
2 Atticus moves to prevent this and enlists the help of Mr Underwood
3 The mob arrives
4 The children appear on the scene
5 The mob disperses

Stage 2
1 *Atticus is told that a mob may try to kill Tom Robinson*
(Maycomb citizens visit Atticus — advice of Link Deas — trouble when Tom Robinson is moved to Maycomb — Jem feels concern for his father's safety.)

2 *Atticus moves to prevent this and enlists the help of Mr Underwood*
(Goes to Tribune office — enlists the help of Mr Underwood — to fire shots at first sign of trouble — Atticus drives out of town in his Chevrolet — tries to fool his children — sits outside jailhouse reading by the light of an extension cord.)

3 *The mob arrives*
(Dusty cars – angry men – Atticus folds paper – pushes hat back – fear – apprehension – tells them the sheriff is nearby.)

4 *Children arrive on the scene*
(Children arrive on the scene – Atticus feels anger and embarrassment – Scout kicks one of the lynch mob – mentions Mr Cunningham's entailment – Mr Cunningham ashamed – situation defuses itself.)

5 *The mob disperses*
(Mob begins to disperse – emotions felt by Atticus – lesson to be learnt – courage – compassion.)

In this assignment you have been asked to write from Atticus's point of view so you must make careful notes about how you think he would have *felt* as the events occurred. Try and see the story through Atticus's eyes. Carefully note down any emotions of fear, anger, pride, embarrassment that you think he may have experienced.

The following is the kind of answer you should aim at from the expansion and development of notes.

> Only one night remained before the trial and I decided to accept the advice of Mr Link Deas. There was no way in which I was going to let a blood-thirsty gang of racial bigots murder Tom: I was sure he was innocent and by heck I was going to prove it! Just because reasonable people go stark raving mad when anything involving a negro comes up there's no excuse for a lawyer to fail in his duty. I'd gone into The Tribune office and Mr Underwood had agreed to help me. He suffered from the usual Maycomb disease, bigotry and hatred of negroes, but at heart he was a decent enough, law-abiding citizen and didn't want a lynching anymore than I did. He was to watch through the window of his office and fire warning shots with his shotgun at the first sign of trouble.
>
> I didn't want the children exposed to any violence so I tried to get them to bed early and pretended I was driving out of town in the Chevrolet. Taking a bulb and a long extension cord, I picked up a paper and tried to make myself comfortable, but I found it hard to concentrate – my eyes just didn't seem to focus on the words, my mouth began to feel dry with tension. What was I doing here? I should have been thinking about the children, this wasn't my fight. Suddenly my thoughts were interrupted by the arrival of four dusty cars. I slowly rose to my feet, 'Here they come,' I thought. My hands began to shake and I could feel a knot of apprehension in my stomach. I shouted to Tom through the bars, trying to inject a note of confidence into my voice.

As the angry group stepped from their cars, I became more worried. 'What was I doing,' I thought, 'I've lived in Maycomb all my life, I know these people, there's still time for me to get away, after all, I had made a gesture – nobody could say I hadn't at least tried.' Then I began to feel more calm. I wasn't the one who was mad, this bunch of vicious, angry men were the ones who were insane. I wasn't going to allow this blind, savage mob to cruelly hang a man who I was convinced was innocent. I began to feel angry. 'Just who did these people think they were?' Anger and fear surged within me. I realized I shouldn't let them see me frightened, that would be the end of everything.

Folding my paper I dropped it in my lap, casually pushing my hat back as the men approached. They ordered me out of the way and I knew that real trouble wasn't far off. I tried a bluff by telling them the sheriff was nearby, but this didn't seem to make much of an impression. Except for Mr Underwood, I was completely at their mercy, alone and unarmed. The only thing left was for me to try and talk them out of it.

Suddenly, to my utter astonishment, Scout burst on the scene shouting out my name. I was completely dumbfounded as Jem and Dill followed close behind. Twin emotions of anger and embarrassment surged through me. Just what were the children doing here? They were sure to get hurt. I didn't want them to witness a man's violent death. I felt sick with embarrassment as I began to realize these men would think I was using the children to prevent an ugly incident – how could Scout and Jem do this to me? I'd never be able to look these people in the eyes again. I ordered Jem to take Scout home at once, but it didn't seem to get through to him. Jem just stood there in a proud, defiant manner. There was no doubt about it, I could see myself in him. He was just as stubborn and difficult as me. I began to get more angry as he persisted in remaining, but there seemed no way in which I would be able to get him to move. One of the men grabbed him by the collar and tried to pull him out of the way. At this, Scout gave the man a really nasty kick and he let go. My goodness, what a thump! I began to feel proud of both of them, and my initial anger and irritation subsided. Scout, recognizing Mr Cunningham, began to talk to him. Brave and innocent as she was, she didn't seem to realize what was happening. 'Hey, Mr Cunningham, how are you getting along with your entailment?' The father of Walter Cunningham seemed really taken aback by this, he was clearly embarrassed by the child's knowledge of his financial and legal affairs. He pretended he didn't know her, but Scout persisted in talking to him. Everyone, myself included, seemed astonished at the child's concern and nerve. At last, her persistence forced Mr Cunningham to acknowledge her. He bent down and spoke to her. He'd obviously been ashamed to let the others know that he'd had dealings with a lawyer defending a negro who'd raped a white girl.

This seemed to bring the men to their senses and took the steam out of the situation. One by one they began to shuffle away.

As individuals, most of them were kindly, decent men, but they had been overtaken by events. Decades of bigotry, racial intolerance and deep seated, irrational hatred had influenced them. As a mob they seemed groups of mindless killers lusting for a man's death, but as ordinary family men they shuffled off to their homes. The Cunninghams knew they were beaten, they wouldn't be able to do anything with the children there. I felt ten foot high. My children had given these men an astonishing demonstration of courage and compassion, a lesson I hoped most of them would never forget. The adult world was probably still just as confusing to Scout, but she was learning to look at life through the eyes of other people. She still had a long way to go, but Scout was learning to make her own decisions, she'd never fall victim to the blind hatred and intolerance of people like the Cunninghams.

A surge of relief charged through my body. In the space of half an hour I'd felt fear, anger, embarrassment, pride and astonishment. I reassured Tom, shouting out that everything was going to be all right, I could sense his relief. The only disappointed person seemed Mr Underwood, who hadn't had the opportunity to use his shotgun. What a day – hatred and intolerance overthrown by courage and innocence; I retired to bed a very humble and proud man.

The writer in this piece of coursework has amply demonstrated a detailed and first-hand knowledge of the text: we note the warning from Mr Link Deas, the details concerning the bulb and extension link, Mr Underwood's offer of help, the arrival of the lynch mob, Scout's confrontation with Mr Cunningham. Such expressions as 'just because reasonable people go stark raving mad' and 'the usual Maycomb disease' are drawn from the novel and reveal something of the candidate's attempt to convey the general flavour of the book. The writer has obviously studied the text carefully and structured the assignment accordingly. Nevertheless, the person marking the coursework will be looking for more than mere narrative recall. Firstly, has the candidate shown an imaginative insight into Atticus's predicament? Has there been any attempt to express what is felt and what is imagined? Secondly, has the writer of this coursework demonstrated an informed personal response to some of the themes and ideas projected in the novel, *To Kill a Mockingbird*? In judging the merit of this answer we should consider some of the following points.

The first thing to note is that the candidate writes in the first person and employs a colloquial form of expression using contractions such as 'didn't' and 'wasn't'. In the past, this kind of informal writing was reserved for direct speech and personal letters: all examination boards now accept that a slightly less formal approach in coursework is perfectly permissible if it helps to convey the candidate's own imaginative insight more effectively.

Writing in a slightly more colloquial manner does not excuse poor grammar. Candidates will be penalized if they are unable to exercise control over the conventions of spelling, punctuation, sentence structure and paragraphing.

Because the writer is writing in the first person a feeling of direct involvement is apparent. There is an effort to convey some of the mixed emotions which Atticus feels as he waits for the mob – 'my hands began to shake and I could feel a knot of apprehension in my stomach' – his embarrassment as the children appear – 'how could Scout and Jem do this to me.' The passive role of the reader has been abandoned and the candidate has demonstrated a convincing understanding of Atticus's emotions of fear, anger, embarrassment, pride and astonishment. This is what the examiner is looking for. *A candidate should be able to communicate a sensitive, sensible, personal response to what is read.*

This coursework also demonstrates a knowledge of some of the underlying themes and ideas of the novel. The idea of 'education' as a theme is well illustrated by the comment '. . . Scout . . . was learning to look at life through the eyes of other people;' the whole concept of moral and physical courage is amply demonstrated. Other ideas the writer seems aware of are man's inhumanity to man and the relationship between parents and children. The writer of this coursework has clearly shown more than a mere surface understanding of events, a much deeper awareness of themes and attitudes has been demonstrated. This is the kind of *informed personal response* the examiner is searching for.

This, then, would have been a very good assignment because the writer has (a) shown an understanding of the text of *To Kill a Mockingbird*; (b) shown a deeper understanding of some of the themes and attitudes; (c) has communicated a sensitive, sensible personal response and has written a good, clear, well-structured and grammatical account.

Note that the mere factual recall of events is *not* enough. By linking these events with an *informed understanding* of the central character's feelings and emotions you are demonstrating the kind of *personal response* and *imaginative insight* which the GCSE literature examination encourages.

Make a detailed summary of the plot of *To Kill a Mockingbird*. Make sure that you have noted the following points and the *significance* of each (i.e. in terms of plot, but also in terms of character and situation, incidents in themselves being the major part of plot). You should be able to indicate the parts played by Jem and Dill in Scout's story, the warmth of the relationship between Scout and her father, the nature of Atticus himself, and the role played by the Radleys, and particularly of Arthur (Boo) Radley in what happens. Consider what they find in the knot-hole of the tree. Then consider the children's relationship with their neighbours, and incidents involving those neighbours who influence the children, such as Miss Maudie, who admires Atticus but whose house burns down, and Mrs Dubose, the morphine taker who suffers agonies but dies bravely in her attempts to break the habit. You might consider the influence on Scout of her coloured housekeeper Calpurnia, her first taste of racial prejudice in the form of her cousin Francis, whom she fights. All these things are related to the main humanitarian themes of the novel. They constitute Scout's real education in life which is to come to the full with the trial and sentence of Tom Robinson, and the latter's death when he tries to escape. Earlier than these events, she has seen the father whom she thought of as rather 'feeble' shoot a mad dog. This incident in itself was preparation for his standing alone against the 'madness' present in Maycomb during the trial. 'One-shot Finch' kills the case against Tom Robinson by a clear demonstration of his innocence, but the madness of bigotry persists, and the white jury ensures that the black man is convicted. The plot provides a number of possible assignments because of its natural connection with themes and characters. It also offers a number of imaginative opportunities for the student who gets really involved in the text. For instance, one of the main mysteries of the novel surrounds Boo Radley, and his role is not clear until the very end. Imagine that you are Boo. Keep a diary of how you kept watch on the Finch house, saying exactly what you did and when before the killing of Bob Ewell. Or imagine you are the sheriff Heck Tate. After you have removed the knife which Ewell had, go home and tell your wife what you have done and what motivated you to do it. Refer to any incident in the novel in which you were involved if it helps your explanation.

Apply the principles demonstrated here to any book you are studying. If you know the plot, you know perhaps the main areas of significance in the book. Plots have sudden twists, secrets, instances of fate or coincidence, the unexpected, the unlikely, the sad, the funny, the sentimental, the melodramatic, the tragic, and many others. You must know clearly what your particular novel has in it if you are to write with any confidence and authority.

Characterization

This is quite simply the ways in which writers present characters in fiction. We can discover what an individual is like by considering the following points:

what the character does; what he says and the way he says it; the character's thoughts and emotions; what other people say about him; what people think about him.

It is not always easy for you to separate plot and characterization. Writers usually present their characters in two ways:

(a) An easily recognizable and predictable character, often a caricature i.e. they have one or two features which are exaggerated to an unnatural degree, e.g. Boxer in George Orwell's *Animal Farm*.

(b) A character who develops as the novel progresses, who learns from experience and who is sometimes unpredictable in behaviour e.g. Bathsheba Everdene in Thomas Hardy's *Far From The Madding Crowd*.

The main idea in considering characterization is that we are looking at the author's attempt to make that character have recognizable human qualities.

In the novel *Shane* by Jack Shaefer, the hero is portrayed in great detail. The desperation of his moves, the sureness of his attack, his brutality, all mark him as a man possessed by some horror from the past. Yet, this man who moves with the ease 'of a coiled spring', typifying hardness, endurance and quiet power, is also a source of comfort, guidance and advice. He is a man who is infinitely gentle and patient. The reader sees his character through the eyes of a young boy and, like Bob Starrett, should be sensitive to the awe, mysterious wonder and love which this compelling character displays. In the same way we see Atticus Finch (*To Kill a Mockingbird*) through the eyes of others. He is not only a figure of reason and maturity, but is presented as a man possessing individuality of action and outlook; a person with a warm sense of humour, courage, affection and loyalty, free from the prejudices of his contemporaries.

In the following example, given in note form, a candidate has been asked to write a typical coursework assignment which requires a set of character studies on some of the more interesting animals in George Orwell's *Animal Farm*. This will not of course be as direct as writing a portrait of Charlotte Brontë's Rochester or Laurie Lee's Uncle Ray. The personalities of Orwell's animals are really part of his political satire, and the candidate must bear this in mind throughout his answer. However, although Orwell does not develop his characters, he does slowly reveal them. In the following piece of coursework the candidate has made an attempt not only to describe the personalities of the animals in detail, but also to relate them to the story. Again, you should notice that the title calls for an imaginative and personalized response on the part of the writer. You will note for instance, the frequent references to ideas such as 'propaganda', 'essential mistruths', 'slight distortions', 'bloody trials' and 'fraternization', which help to convey something of the nature of political dishonesty.

Assignment

'These scenes of terror and slaughter were not what they had looked forward to on that night when Old Major had first stirred them to rebellion.' Taking Boxer, Napoleon, Benjamin, Clover and Moses the Raven as examples, compile Squealer's secret police reports on them.

Boxer
Owing to his massive strength and alleged steadiness of character, the horse Boxer enjoys enormous popularity on the farm. We pigs, however, have mixed feelings about his loyalty. Suffers from lack of intelligence – Naive questioning of simple change – Blind regard for welfare of other animals – Efforts have been made to discipline him – Secret police unsuccessful – Punishment has been deferred.

Weakness lies in blind and innocent regard for Comrade Napoleon – 'Napoleon is always right' – For the time being we have need of his strength – But when the time comes we pigs have long memories . . .

Napoleon
Never mixes with any other animals – Mysterious figure of awe and terror – Understands the value of propaganda – and effective planning – It was he who made the revolution and formed his bodyguard – He alone understands that the future of Animalism lies in our hands – Cannot afford luxury of moral scruples – Slight distortions and essential mistruths are necessary from time to time.

His weakness lies in his vanity – Likes to be referred to as the 'Fountain of Happiness' – Loves adulation. Animals are unaware he is responsible for their sixty-hour week – It was he who starved the chickens and organized the bloody trials. Is getting more like Farmer Jones each day. Napoleon is a cunning creature who makes a dangerous and vindictive enemy . . .

Clover
Stout motherly mare approaching middle life – Weak and sentimental regard for others – Failed to report a dangerous act of fraternization by Mollie, who is a danger to all of us. Has been known to make unfavourable comparisons between old days of cruelty and hardship and new era of happiness and contentment. Has been seen talking with dangerous and cynical Benjamin. She is an animal who will have to be carefully watched.

Moses the Raven
A spy and tale-bearer who does no work. Before revolution lived on the bread and beer which our enemy Farmer Jones provided. He is a hireling and agent – Clever and cunning creature – Refutes our teachings – Corrupts our comrades with tales of a paradise called Sugarcandy Mountain.

Spreads lies and confusion, yet is tolerated. Why is it that Comrade Napoleon allows him to live? What is his secret?

Benjamin
Bad-tempered donkey who possesses a cynical disregard for our new order – His carping remarks do nothing to inspire our comrades – Constantly belittles our great steps forward – Cannot accept that we can achieve a paradise on earth – Insists our comrades' social conditions will not change – Only great age and his close association with Old Major prevent us from dealing with him . . .

A novel stands or falls by the quality of its characterization, and as you study your novels and stories and write about them you will find that certain characters come alive for you by the individuality they possess. We have already observed that there are developing characters in fiction, just as we ourselves develop in life. They, and we, have certain psychological traits and truths. We mentioned Bathsheba Everdene in Thomas Hardy's *Far From the Madding Crowd*. This young woman moves from vanity and condescension to a whimsical action which changes the course of her life just as we, when we make decisions (or back away from them) are changing the direction of our own lives. Bathsheba, on the toss of a coin, sends a valentine with the seal MARRY ME to a reticent and distant farmer neighbour of hers who has apparently had an unhappy love affair. Boldwood, unaware that this was mere whimsy, responds in an impassioned manner and implores Bathsheba to fulfil her offer. Hardy is showing character in action and development. We should not have expected that Boldwood had these hidden depths, but that is what character is like and that is precisely what Hardy is displaying. Bathsheba's half promises to Boldwood are more seriously misplaced when she falls in love with Sergeant Troy, an opportunist who has already seduced a young local girl, Fanny Robin. The student of human nature will find Bathsheba's behaviour in setting off to Bath to give up her lover and ending up by marrying him to be irrational but recognizably human. Bathsheba now has to go through the painful process of discovering what her husband is like. Troy disappears but, though presumed dead, returns to the neighbourhood intending to claim Bathsheba – after all, she is his wife and she has enough money for him to support himself. When he does return and tries to compel Bathsheba he is shot dead by Boldwood – that impassioned nature can take no more. When Bathsheba finally marries Gabriel Oak, who has loved her selflessly and loyally through all these trials and tribulations, she is much more soberly ready to spend her life with him. There is no reduction of Bathsheba. When Troy is shot she lays out his body although she has had no experience of a like situation; yet such is the consistency of her character that she goes to Oak and virtually proposes to him just as earlier she had proposed to the ill-fated Boldwood. The reader of this brief summary of her character will note Hardy's adherence to the *psychological truth* of his presentation.

Far From the Madding Crowd, a novel of English nineteenth-century village and agricultural life, was published in 1874. Almost 100 years later, in fact in 1968, Barry Hines, who was born in a village near Barnsley in Yorkshire, wrote *A Kestrel for a Knave*, which became a successful film. It is not our intention here to compare the two novels, which are set in different areas in different times of the development of our society. We are concerned here with characterization of a compelling and disturbing kind. Billy Casper is a boy from a broken home. He is under-sized, under-nourished, cheeky, has delinquent tendencies, a brutal and bullying brother and a promiscuous mother. He is a survivor, a thief, without direction in life. He is ill-clothed (he has no PE or football kit, and is the butt of the other boys and of a sadistic member of staff) and unloved. During the novel's action he only establishes human contact with one other person, and that is the sympathetic English master Mr Farthing who, unexpectedly, takes an interest in Billy's training of his hawk. But Billy does make human contact of a unique and loving kind. He acquires the hawk mentioned above, calls it Kes, trains it, worships it, takes pride in it, steals for it. Kes gives reality and meaning to Billy's life. He is dedicated, ecstatic, absorbed; the bird does what education fails to do, what a sordid life can never do. It gives Billy a reason for living. Both here and away from the bird Billy is a totally convincing character. This is because Barry Hines has succeeded in presenting him from within. He knows that the small world in which Billy lives is against him, and Billy knows it too. Billy tells lies, he fails to place Jud's bet (with tragic consequences), he clowns in goal, scratching his armpits and imitating a monkey. But Billy is not caricature – he is the genuine product of his home and environment. When he steals Kes and makes her his own he is rebelling against the frustrations of his meaningless existence at school and at home. He is a loner, outsider, easily picked on, and there is no more moving revelation of character than when Billy writes 'A Tall Story' in which he pathetically reveals what he would like to have instead of his present mutilating reality. He longs for a large house on the moors, he wants to have breakfast in bed (gone would be the desultory paper-round he is forced to do), and he wants his father back (of course as he remembered him). His fear of Jud is seen in the fact that he would like him to be permanently in the army, he would like all the teachers to be nice to him, his mother would be at home all the time and he would have fish and chips for supper. But Barry Hines does not distort the presentation; Billy can't spell, his writing is undisciplined, yet the clear wish-fulfilment comes across with an immediate poignancy.

Scarred physically and morally, Billy has the capacity to endure. But his character cannot be measured by the conventional standards, for by those measures he is both a failure and an outcast. In short, his taking of Kes is the beginning of his education, his training of her is his morality, her murder the reassertion of his disillusion. Barry Hines does not duck the issues raised by Billy's life through a happy ending. We are left with the certainty that Billy will continue to be victim, outsider, delinquent. Though he is strongly individualized Billy is a symbol too for all those like him. And, as with Hardy in Bathsheba, we are aware of the psychological truth to life of the portrayal.

The object here of showing you two successfully and convincingly presented characters is to make you think about the nature of character itself in fiction. If you are studying either of the two novels mentioned above, you will be able to assess your judgement of character against the one we have given above – adding in points or character traits that we have missed, or considering those characters we have only mentioned in passing. If you have not studied either of the books, look closely at the characters in the books you are studying, and ask yourself relevant questions about them. You might consider the following:

(a) is each character true to life?

(b) are they presented with consistency?

(c) are they the products of their environment, their particular kinds of families (poor, rich, middle-class, social status, professional etc)?

(d) has the character any abnormal traits, strong views or prejudices, mental, emotional or physical disabilities etc?

(e) what do other people think of the character (close relations, friends, even enemies)?

(f) is the character egoistic or unselfish, or both?

(g) how much of the character's reactions are revealed through (a) unspoken thoughts or emotions or (b) his or her own words?

(h) do you find the character sympathetic or not? Give reasons for your answer.

(i) write down the crises or dramatic situations in which the character is involved. What do his/her reactions to these situations tell you?

(j) list brief quotations which reveal what the character is like.

Assignment

Compare and contrast the characters of Rochester and St John Rivers in *Jane Eyre or* compare and contrast any two major characters in a novel you are studying.

Notes

Introduction   Brief outline of who Rochester is – past history – owner of Thornfield – love for Jane – St John Rivers – clergyman – repression of feelings – cold – driven by duty – love for Jane.

Para 2   Physical contrasts of the two men – Rochester strong – athletic – not handsome – powerful – St John – 'handsome featured face' – 'like chiselled marble' (other points on both men with particular mention of eyes).

Para 3   Contrasts of temperament – personality – character etc – Rochester – confesses his past (most of it) to Jane – impulsive – generous – impassioned though initially gruff – moody – impressionable (re Jane) – tender – anguished – jealous.

Para 4   St John – cold (give example) – conscientious – dutiful – ambitious (in his own chosen way) – represses love and attraction (for Rosamond Oliver) – strong sense of vocation – strong-willed – self-denying *but* sacrifices others to his needs (and would do Jane) – prepared for suffering – even enjoys prospect of martyrdom.

Para 5   Return to Rochester – insecure because of his secret – motive in having house party (to drive Jane mad with jealousy) – shows initiative (disguises himself as gipsy) – some sadism here – selfish, man of action (the marriage) – but after injuries somewhat changed, emphasize that he is a physical wreck – but proud, arrogant at times, teasing, intelligent, sometimes brusque, always human.

Para 6   St John again – fanatical – seen in demands he makes on Jane – uses her – plays on her sense of duty – no respect for her feelings – moral and spiritual blackmail – pride – obstinacy – cannot be crossed – yet scrupulous – kind to sisters – severe, incapable of an intimate relationship – lacks humility.

Conclusion   (perhaps) Rochester more human despite faults – Charlotte Brontë's achievement in their presentation – the outwardly not so attractive man appealing and compelling – the attractive man unlikeable – warm and cold, heart and head contrast.

Character is at the heart of all fiction, and our headings like 'Plot', 'Themes', 'Setting' etc cannot be separated in *your* writing from the integral presence of the characters. The latter make up the *plot*, are seen against the *setting* and embody the *theme* or *themes* (or contradict them) and, taken with these other aspects, constitute the structure of the novel.

Setting

Setting is concerned with the physical background or a particular time in which the action takes place. This background to the novel is vital because, unless it is created convincingly, neither plots nor characters are convincing. The setting for Barry Hines's *A Kestrel For a Knave* is completely real because the novel is set in an area which the author knows well. The setting of *To Kill a Mockingbird* is the pre-war Deep South of the United States, consisting not only of a physical description of Maycomb, but of all the religious bigotry, racial intolerance, fear and ignorance which are a part of this 'tired old town' set like 'an island in a patchwork sea of cotton fields'.

During the course of *Jane Eyre*, the rich and eccentric Rochester proposes to the heroine. The setting is the magnificent garden of his house, Thornfield, on a beautiful midsummer's eve. The writer of the assignment has been asked to look back on this 'enchanted evening' and re-live this memory through the eyes of the lonely, blinded Rochester. Naturally, the setting of the occasion would be most important. The emotional impact of the scene is enhanced by the characters' perception of the beauty around them. If you look at the following sample assignment which is included in note form, you will notice that the student has used many examples from the text to illustrate this fact. You will notice the reference to the 'sun sinking in simple state,' the clouds glowing with 'solemn purple,' the 'light of red jewels' which light up the hill tops. Likewise, the fragrance of the flowers and Rochester's cigar, the bright colours of the moth and the sweet sound of the nightingale provide a suitable setting for this proposal. The writer of the assignment also indicates how, during the course of the evening, the weather changes as if displaying some symbolic anger at Rochester's behaviour; even the great horse-chestnut tree under which the bigamous proposal is made, is blasted by lightning. This assignment, though tackled in a highly personalized manner, has accurately recounted the event, and shown some awareness of the novel's deeper themes.

Assignment

After carefully reading the whole of Chapter 23 of *Jane Eyre*, describe in detail the enchanted evening when Jane agrees to become the wife of Edward Fairfax Rochester. How might Rochester remember these events as he sadly waits for death much later in his gloomy mansion, Ferndean.

Notes

Para 1 It all seemed so long ago – strong scent of my cigar – soft midsummer eve – sun sinking in simple state – clouds glowed with solemn purple – light of red jewels touch the hilltop – a solitary star seemed to light up the orchard – appearance of Jane – fragrance of flowers – sight of the beautiful moth – sunset meeting with moonrise.

Para 2 The joke about Jane being sent to Ireland – We would never meet again – Sadness in Jane's face – 'I grieve to leave Thornfield: I love Thornfield: I love it because I have lived in it a full and delightful life' – Satisfaction at Jane's distress when she thought I might be marrying Blanche Ingram – That she couldn't stay at Thornfield without me – wind wafting through the laurels – Far away the nightingale could still be heard.

Para 3 Pride and delight as she accepts my proposal – 'You – poor and obscure, and small and plain as you are – I entreat to accept me as a husband.' Fear and foreboding as I remember my position – Gloom of my thoughts seemed to find an echo in nature – blind howls and shrieks in the chestnut tree – Lightning tore at my tree – My hopes were at an end.

This is external setting, with the assignment drawing on knowledge of the text, and more importantly the candidate's imaginative identification with one of the main characters in the novel. The assignment here is shorter than some already undertaken, since the work in your file will be both varied and of varied length. It focuses sharply on the scene, and the writer has his overall knowledge of the book as well as his detailed reading of Chapter 23 to help him in framing the particular mood. We have indicated that in all aspects of fictional study character will be pre-eminent, as indeed it is here, but the combination of setting and mood is a commonplace in fiction.

Consider the importance of setting in William Golding's novel, *Lord of the Flies* which was first published in 1954 and has become one of the classics of our own time and probably for all time. The boys are plane-wrecked on a Pacific island, and therefore are isolated from the civilization which has conditioned them. They elect a chief, and at first live amicably. But soon differences arise among them as to priorities, the veneer of their civilized behaviour wears thin, they have nightmares and fears in this unfamiliar place, and eventually their group splits into two sections – those who hunt and become savages and *kill* and those – eventually only Ralph remains – who believe in rational conduct and the moral codes of their past. Golding uses setting here to underline change, treating it paradisiacally and realistically at the same time. The chapter headings alone (*Fire on the Mountain, Huts on the Beach, Beast from Water Castle Rock*) are all ironic comments on the changes and perspectives which the translation of the boys to the island has brought about. Against this foreground the little English boys become little savages, almost as if the savages who at one time must have inhabited the island have been reborn. Setting is used here to express change but also to underline the twentieth-century change in its attitudes towards children and their reactions. By re-invoking R. M. Ballantyne's nineteenth-century boys' adventure story *The Coral Island* Golding is demonstrating that boys were thought of with a certain naiveté. For example, in Ballantyne's story the boys succeed in fending for themselves. They are not put out by the setting but embrace it as a kind of adventure and challenge. Realism is non-existent, natives and pirates feature prominently, the boys act with the heroism of idealized men, the characters are black and white (in the non-racist sense of that term) and all ends happily.

In *Lord of the Flies* the setting is at first illusory (that is, it seems made for good and responsible scout-like activities and commitment) but it becomes importantly realistic. The death of Simon and the prelude to it demonstrate the primary place of setting in Golding's vision – clouds build up over the island, Simon goes up the mountain to see the 'beast', frees the parachute from the rocks, then staggers down the mountain to tell the others what he has found. Simon crawls out of the jungle into the terrifying ritualistic 'party', and is slaughtered, while the wind lifts and carries the parachute and its burden out to sea. From the setting Golding conjures a mystical and beautiful aftermath to this terror as the body of Simon moves out to sea.

Setting is often used at the opening of a book – it provides a natural introduction – often being the background and the foreground against which characters have their being. Read the following opening extract from Steinbeck's *Of Mice and Men*.

A few miles south of Soledad, the Salinas River drops in close to the hill-side bank and runs deep and green. The water is warm too, for it has slipped twinkling over the yellow sands in the sunlight before reaching the narrow pool. On one side of the river the golden foothills curve up to the strong and rocky Gabilan mountains, but on the valley side the water is lined with trees – willows fresh and green with every spring, carrying in their lower leaf junctures the debris of the winter's flooding; and sycamores with mottled, white, recumbent limbs and branches that arch over the pool. On the sandy bank under the trees the leaves lie deep and so crisp that a lizard makes a great skittering if he runs among them. Rabbits come out of the brush to sit on the sand in the evening, and the damp flats are covered with the night tracks of 'coons, and with the spread pads of dogs from the ranches, and with the split-wedge tracks of deer that come to drink in the dark.

There is a path through the willows and among the sycamores, a path beaten hard by boys coming down from the ranches to swim in the deep pool, and beaten hard by tramps who come wearily down from the highway in the evening to jungle-up near water. In front of the low horizontal limb of a giant sycamore there is an ash-pile made by many fires; the limb is worn smooth by men who have sat on it.

Evening of a hot day started the little wind to moving among the leaves. The shade climbed up the hills toward the top. On the sand-banks the rabbits sat as quietly as little grey, sculptured stones. And then from the direction of the state highway came the sound of footsteps on crisp sycamore leaves. The rabbits hurried noiselessly for cover. A stilted heron laboured up into the air and pounded down river. For a moment the place was lifeless, and then two men emerged from the path and came into the opening by the green pool. They had walked in single file down the path, and even in the open one stayed behind the other. Both were dressed in denim trousers and in denim coats with brass buttons. Both wore shapeless black hats and both carried tight blanket rolls slung over their shoulders. The first man was small and quick, dark of face, with restless eyes and sharp, strong features. Every part of him was defined: small, strong hands, slender arms, a thin and bony nose. Behind him walked his opposite, a huge man, shapeless of face, with large, pale eyes, with wide, sloping shoulders; and he walked heavily, dragging his feet a little, the way a bear drags his paws. His arms did not swing at his sides, but hung loosely and only moved because the heavy hands were pendula.

This passage lends itself to a number of assignments, and you should bring to it the careful reading which has been recommended throughout this book. Work through it after a first reading to get the sense and the atmosphere, and pay particular attention to the following:

(a) What kind of atmosphere does the author create here? (You should pay particular attention to the detailed description of nature and the general effect of the scene. Notice particularly the effect of silence.)

(b) Pick out particular words and phrases which seem to you to be vividly descriptive.

(c) Make a list of the *images* (similes and metaphors). In what ways do they enhance the effect of the author's writing?

(d) In what ways is this a loving and nostalgic piece of writing? Quote phrases or sentences from the text which show that the author knows the place well – you should pay particular attention to accuracy, familiarity and tone in the writing.

(e) The author makes use of personification and onomatopoeia. Pick out examples of these and say what they contribute to the atmosphere and tone of the passage.

(f) Show how the author uses contrast both in his descriptions of nature and of the two men.

The questions above should, when they are answered, show that you have understood the passage and that you have the capacity to appreciate the writer's art in it.

Assignments

NOW if you have read the book, undertake the following:

1 Show what part setting plays in *Of Mice and Men*, referring particularly to the natural background, the ranch and, specifically, the barn.

2 Compare and contrast George and Lennie. For whom do you feel the most sympathy and why?

3 Write an account of the most dramatic incident in the novel, bringing out clearly the importance of the location where it occurs.

Notes to question 3

Suggested heading: *The killing of Curley's wife.*

Introduction Setting for dramatic incident – the barn on Sunday afternoon – restful horses – flies – afternoon sun – outside noises of men – Lennie in barn looking at dead puppy – his pathetic talk to it – significance of this in view of what is to happen.

Para 2   Lennie's reactions (i) what he will tell George (ii) blind anger (significance) – entrance of Curley's wife – physical description – what she says to Lennie – Curley's injury (significance) – her approach to Lennie.

Para 3   Her loneliness – her need to talk – Lennie easily responding (despite the fact that he knows he shouldn't talk to her) – the uncovering of the dead puppy – sympathetic reassurance of Curley's wife – her defensive-aggressiveness in conversation – her confiding in Lennie re Curley.

Para 4   Description of wall, horses – sun – build-up of tension – the girl's baiting of Lennie – rabbits – his moving close against her – her calling him 'nuts' – his stroking her hair – 'Lennie was in a panic' – his hand over her mouth and nose – his pleading with her – her struggles – THEN

Para 5   Detail on what Lennie actually does – the killing – 'for Lennie had broken her neck' – the pathos of 'I done a bad thing. I done another bad thing'. Focus on barn, covering of hay, cry of men outside the barn – Lennie peering out through the cracks of the barn – the dead puppy

Conclusion   The importance of the setting – the atmosphere inside the barn – the feeling of being cut off from others – the non-communication between Lennie and the girl – the build-up of tension – the closeness – gentleness into violence. Stress Steinbeck's techniques and the sympathy for Lennie even at the moment of killing.

If you have NOT read the book, write an assignment on one of the following:

1 Taking the passage from *Of Mice and Men* as a starting point, write about the importance of setting (obviously with character in mind as well) in the novel or novels and stories you are studying. You might stress how the author writes in terms of a natural setting or, for example, of an urban setting or describe any interior settings (particular places or rooms) which are important in the development of the plot.

2 Sometimes the author will use contrasting settings as, for example, Emily Brontë does in *Wuthering Heights*, where the house is used as a symbolic and factual contrast with Thrushcross Grange. Write about contrasting locations in any one of the books or stories you are studying.

3 In the Steinbeck extract, humanity appears upon the scene in the form of the two men, later identified as George and Lennie. From one of the books studied, describe how a character or characters is in sympathy with his or her background. If a character or characters in one of your books finds the physical background of home, work etc unsympathetic or the cause of conflict, then say in what ways the particular background influences the character's thoughts and actions.

4 Imagine you are a character in one of the books you are studying. Write a letter to a friend describing what you feel about where you live or work, bringing out the good points and the bad points which you find either in your immediate environment or in the countryside around you.

Setting in place has been stressed, but setting in time (which obviously involves place) is of equal importance. One aspect of twentieth-century writing which merits close attention is the novel which deals with the threats which the nuclear age has brought with it. There are obviously variants on the situation, for example in John Wyndham's *The Day of the Triffids*, where blindness is the order of the day, and where the scientific ramifications are frightening in their widespread intensity. Even more frightening in its analysis of human nature against a setting in time is John Christopher's *The Death of Grass* (1956) in which the Chung-li virus of the 1950s kills grass and all related plant-forms – like wheat, oats etc, thus depriving humans and animals of food with a resultant famine. The Far East is devastated, science finds counter-viruses which successively fail, governments – like the British government – are bent on atomic destruction of the majority in order to save the minority. John Christopher's setting is the world, but he narrows down the human reaction to a small group of Southerners, tracing their flight from London, their journey northwards towards the haven of a valley which has such a narrow pass that it can be easily defended. The nature of this valley is described through a cunning use of retrospect, with the two brothers visiting it with their widowed mother. Both become in their different ways attracted to it. David inherits it much later from his grandfather, who had determined that he would have it; John has a strange adventure as a child there, falling into the River Lepe which runs underground for part of its course. He is carried through on the current and out into the daylight again. Most importantly, he has found that there is a shelf in the middle of the river, and this has prevented him from drowning. Later that shelf is to prove of vital importance as John and the redoubtable Pirrie attack the stockade *from the river* in order to enter the valley, which in turn will protect them from attack.

This setting contrasts with the London and southern settings of the early part of the novel. Strangely, like William Golding two years before him, John Christopher explores human nature in crisis, the crisis of adversity which causes man to revert to instinctive and primitive behaviour. Just as the boys on the island reveal the beast in their natures, so the adults in *The Death of Grass*, despite their high degree of civilization, kill to survive, loot and rape in a dying land where self is all and where the weak cannot possibly live. The nightmare world of the novel takes us from setting to setting, with, for example, early in the novel John and his friend Roger discussing the rumours of impending disaster in the interiors of pub and club. Another fine interior is the gunsmith's shop owned by Pirrie, and there are two separate assaults on isolated houses, in which the layout of rooms is important. This focus on interior setting is particularly distinct while exteriors such as road junctions and above all the trek across the Pennines are graphically described together with the killings which are inevitable. With John's party as aggressors, the bodies of a husband and wife killed by them are hurriedly stuffed under the stairs while one of the party reasons with the daughter of the dead couple in an upstairs bedroom. When she agrees to go with her parents' killers we are aware of the setting she is turning her back on forever, typified by the old and blind dog which is left behind.

A novel like *The Death of Grass* can provide the interested student with a number of assignments. In the first instance there is the fearful and terrifying situation. We might ponder on the efficacy of science to provide the right answers always. The Chung-li virus may burn itself out – this is discussed at one stage during the novel – but until it does so or an anti-virus is found the famine will continue. Is it conceivable that a government would order its aircraft to atom and hydrogen bomb its own cities in order to reduce the population? Is human nature as 'survival-selfish' as the groups of people in the novel? Can you imagine yourself as one of these characters? Keep a diary of all that happens from the moment that you set out for the North, bringing in what happens to your friends and family and any new-comers that you meet. If you are one of the children, imagine yourself left behind in the school, and say what happens to you and your friends. You are writing for those who survive this and who have to make a new life in the future. You might draw a map of the journey northwards, together with some notes as an addition to the map, indicating what major incidents occurred on the journey. Or you could write about the incidents in order to show what has happened to human nature as a result of the catastrophe. You might write too about individual characters, comparing Roger – who early on appears to be the leader – with John, who is elected leader on the toss of a coin. You might write about the impact of Mr Pirrie and say whether you approve of what he does. How useful is he during the flight? You could consider the roles of the women characters, comparing Ann and Olivia for example, and indicating the importance of Millicent and Jane. And you could project yourself to the end of the novel, and identify yourself with John – who believes that he has killed his brother or at any rate is responsible for his death – as he says 'There's a lot to do' . . . 'A city to be built'. What do you think he is going to do? Say what he does. Put yourself in his position and make a log of the various tasks he sets himself and others to do, and the priority which they give to them. Or project yourself beyond this, and, as they battle to survive (say how they do this), write an account of news coming in from the outside world and say how this affects those behind the stockade in the valley. This fine novel merits detailed appreciation and interpretation and invites imaginative writing because of the stimulating qualities of imagination displayed in it. It is likely that if you have not read this particular novel you will at least have read one which has similarities or at some stage points of contact with it. If you have, devise your own assignments, or discuss them with your teacher, based on ideas and suggestions found above.

Another novel of this type, where setting is all important, is *Z for Zachariah*. Here the specific and, in terms of the context of the novel, permanent setting is the valley after the nuclear holocaust. Ann Burden (note the name) believes that she is the sole survivor, for everyone in the valley was killed while her parents, who left to investigate what had happened, never returned. The valley is there-fore the be-all and end-all of Ann's existence one year after the catastrophe. The span of the valley only makes the sense of isolation the more complete, for although the valley has escaped the war, one of the two streams has been contaminated. (It may be remarked here in passing that the astute reader will have noticed certain parallels with both *Lord of the Flies* and *The Death of Grass* which have been glanced at during the course of this commentary.) One day on a ridge outside the valley Ann sees smoke. This brings with it hope and fear, the first since this may mean that she will have companionship, the second the possibility of danger. Setting in detail is here given a considered stress. Ann decides to be cautious, makes the farm look uninhabited so that no one will suspect her existence, retires to a cave from where she can see any approach to the farm. The stranger she sees swims in the contaminated Burden Creek, though he later finds the second clean stream. It is not my intention here to dwell on all the details of the plot, but the stranger (ill from radiation sickness) is able to make practical suggestions about the running of the farm. Fields and the interior of the house contribute to the narrative tension of the novel, with the stranger (Mr Loomis) firing a rifle into the house, speaking of noises upstairs, but really in his delirium living through past actions and the consequent guilt. This becomes the major substance of the novel, yet the setting continues in a compulsive way to dominate so much of the action. For example, in the interior Ann is nearly raped by Mr Loomis; she finds refuge in her cave in the exterior. Setting is now equated with fear, as Ann becomes virtually a prisoner in what she had come to think of as her own valley. Eventually Ann decides to leave that valley, Mr Loomis advises her to travel west, and Ann does so, setting out through the unknown and barren landscape in her attempt to find a new life for herself. The impact of the setting, with both space and interior claustrophobic at times, suggests imprisonment of the body and, in the case of Mr Loomis and Ann in different ways, imprisonment of the mind.

Because of the importance of his setting Robert O'Brien has succeeded in giving his novel a powerful directness – he traps the reader into location and narrative just as his characters are so trapped. The result is a single and unswerving narrative tension which is not relaxed until the end of the book when Ann sets off on her journey of hope. There are no sub-plots. Just as Ann's past reaches back into the valley so Mr Loomis's past reaches back into his relationship with and killing of Edward. But both are contained within the ongoing action of time present. Thus the author has structured his novel with a skilful economy, and because the sense of narrative focus and place is so sharp the reader is involved, absorbed all the time. Again, the text provides a number of jumping off points for assignments both in direct appreciation and in imaginative development and association.

Assignments

If candidates have read the book, some of the following assignments, either in controlled conditions or written up over a period of study, could be undertaken:

1 Put yourself in the position of Mr Loomis. Basing your writing on incidents and situations which occur in the book, describe what you do – providing reasons wherever possible – from the time you reach the deserted farmhouse up to your swimming in the radioactive water. You may, like Ann, write this in the form of a diary if you wish.

2 Read Chapter 11 of the novel closely. When you have done so, write a short script for radio about the events leading up to Edward's death. In the course of your writing you may reproduce dialogue from the text of *Z for Zachariah*, but you may make up your own dialogue too, taking it from the description of events given by Ann.

3 Write brief biographies of Ann and Mr Loomis until the time that he appears in the valley. You should use material which is to be found in the novel at different stages. When you have done this, bring out clearly in your writing the ways in which the background of each character differs.

4 What qualities in Ann Burden's character seem to you to be important and why. Before you write your answer, make a careful list of Ann's characteristics, finding in the text references and quotations which support your views. You should also indicate whether she seems to you to have any faults.

5 Since the setting is important to our full appreciation, draw a sketch – or even a sketch-map – of the valley, indicating the important locations with a key which shows where certain incidents took place. (You will need to locate the ridge, farmhouse, the two streams, woods, cave etc.)

6 Read the following passages carefully, and then answer the questions printed below them.

And then, sickeningly, the truth came to me.

The idea, the scene, the things that happened in the next minutes, the next hour, were so bad that I do not like to think about them because they come back to me like a nightmare and I am living them over again.

I am sitting beside the pond with my sock in my hand and my shoe beside me, waiting for my foot to dry. The piece of soap is on a stone at the edge of the water.

And I think: he was not trying to miss. He wants to shoot me in the leg so I cannot walk. He wants to maim, not to kill me. So that he can catch me. It is a simple plan, a terrible one. Starvation will force me to come to the house or the store. And the gun will keep me from going away again. He will try again and again.

And I think: why must he do it?

As I sit there by the pond I hear the tractor start. I know by some instinct before I see it what is going to happen next. I put on my sock and my shoe as fast as I can and run up the hill to the bushes where I hid before.

The tractor, looking bright red in the morning sun, comes out of the trees. On it, as before, holding his gun in his hand, rides Mr Loomis. The gun barrel shines like a tube of blue glass; it is the small rifle, the .22; he does not want to shatter my leg, only cripple it, because after I am caught he intends it to mend again.

(Chapter 23)

(a) What impression does the first passage give you of Ann Burden? Select brief quotations or references to reinforce what you say.

(b) The passage begins in the past tense and then changes into the present tense. Why? What effect is produced by using the present tense?

(c) Why do you think Mr Loomis's treatment of Ann becomes so unpleasant after he recovers from his illness? You may relate this extract to other parts of the novel in your answer.

(d) In what ways is the style of this extract typical of *Z for Zachariah* as a whole? You may quote from other sections of the novel in order to point out comparisons and similarities.

I knew it was the end. I was sixteen and I had worked so hard to keep things going and now I was going to die. A wave of disappointment swept over me, disappointment so bitter it wiped out even my fear. I stood up and faced him. I do not know why he did not shoot me. Instead he saw the safe-suit and began to shout:

'It's mine. You know it's mine. Take it off!'

'No,' I said, 'I won't.'

He aimed the gun at me. I stood still. I could not think what to do, so when words came from my mouth even I was surprised and not conscious of having thought. I realize now they probably saved my life.

'Yes,' I said, 'you can kill me . . . the way you killed Edward.'

(Chapter 26)

(a) How does the author convey the surprise and fear of Mr Loomis?

(b) Select another occasion in the book which shows Ann's courage. Give details of the incident either by reference or quotation, and explain briefly why you have chosen it.

(c) The last thing that Ann says in this extract is vitally important. Say why this is so, and relate it to that part of the novel which makes it so.

(d) Both extracts convey tense situations. Using the atmosphere and the techniques of both, write as if you were Mr Loomis seeking out Ann for a confrontation. Say why you are doing this, and what you hope to get from it. You should refer to any relevant information in the novel in your answer.

Themes

The theme of a novel is often more apparent when an author is commenting on the world in which he lives. In *1984*, for example, Orwell attempts to show us what life would be like in a state-controlled society. In *To Kill a Mockingbird* Harper Lee deals with the relationship between children and parents, man's inhumanity to man, racial bigotry and education. These are ideas which make the novel a coherent whole and give meaning and perspective to the reader's understanding of human behaviour.

In the following example a candidate has been asked to say something about the lessons the young Bob Starrett may have learned during the course of his relationship with his hero, the reformed gunfighter, Shane. One of the basic themes of Jack Shaefer's novel *Shane* is the idea of maturing. The young Bob Starrett experiences complex emotions which, without Shane's visit, he would have been unaware of until much later. The notion that a gun is as good or as bad as the man who uses it is a very mature idea for a boy to grasp. Nevertheless, by the time Shane leaves the valley, we may feel certain that the young Bob is sure to 'grow straight inside as a man should'. Similarly, the idea of choice and decision is a central theme. The writer of this piece of coursework clearly shows this in the first paragraph, and writes of the way in which Shane, randomly choosing one of two trails, picks the trail which brings him into the valley and the lives of everyone who lives there. You should be able to see in this example an awareness of the basic themes and attitudes implicit in the original story, as well as the candidate's attempt to express a sensitive and informed response.

Assignment

'A gun is just a tool . . . It's as good – and as bad – as the man who carries it.' Many years later Bob Starrett reflects on the appearance of the mysterious Shane and considers some of the lessons he learnt as a ten-year old boy. Writing as Bob Starrett, think over some of the major events – what would you have learnt from them?

Suggested note-form answer

I remember that summer of '89, the way he seemed to briefly hesitate before selecting the road which led to our house – If he hadn't picked that road, mine and everyone's life in the valley would have been different – A lean, athletic figure – distant searching eyes – compact energy – his whole being like a coiled spring – the man who came from the west.

What was there about Shane's past which seemed so mysterious and terrifying? – Why did he keep a gun polished in his saddle blanket? – Why was he so silent about his background? – The disappointment when he refused to fight at Grafton's store – The realization, some time later, that it took more courage for him to avoid trouble – When he really had to fight, because there was no other way, he really did fight – He knew my father couldn't fight Fletcher and his men – The deadly efficient way he killed Stark Wilson – Shane's feelings about the range – Shane, the man who wasn't afraid to use his gun as an instrument of justice.

My memories of Shane – Not just a man of violence – He was the man who helped a small boy, even when he was facing possible death himself – The man who helped a faltering boy to look out over the magnificent country and live out his boyhood and grow straight inside as a man should.

Joan Lingard's *Across the Barricades* has the conflict in contemporary Ireland between Protestants and Catholics as its major theme. Although it was first published in 1972, its street, house, family account of the 'troubles' is as vividly recorded as anything we see there now on our television screens. The reader of *Across the Barricades* will find much to write about in terms of coursework assignments. For example, a close look at the novel could stimulate an investigation of the history of the Protestant–Catholic divisions. It would be rewarding to examine the author's use of dialogue and dialect, saying whether or not you find it convincing. But because the novel makes an immediate impact on its readers, fully involving them in the events, the main focus is on the theme of conflict, with its major by-product of mindless, irrational violence and its effect on the characters who are caught up in it. Put briefly, our own interest is drawn to the main characters Sadie Jackson and Kevin McCoy. Both are independent and spirited young people trapped within rigid confines. They fall in love with one another, not merely through physical attraction (though this is part of it) but because each recognizes an essential integrity in the other. They know they will be criticized, they know that they will meet opposition in their families, they know that eyes will watch them in the street, they know they may be threatened. Yet such is their inward courage that the Protestant Sadie and the Catholic Kevin cross the unnatural barricades which are set up against them and their kind. Admittedly, they have to flee to freedom in the end, and by making this the conclusion to her novel Joan Lingard is inviting the reader to think about the unchanging plight of those who remain behind, trapped behind the barricades of bigotry and violence in the names of politics and religion. Read the novel carefully, and then answer the questions of your choice from those listed below. Note that the questions are increasingly challenging.

Assignments

1 In what ways are Sadie and Kevin independent? In your answer quote some of the things they say which tell you what kind of people they are.

2 Compare the Jackson family with the McCoy family. Although they have religious differences, indicate whether you think they have much in common with one another. Again, quote from the text in your answer.

3 Write character sketches of (a) Uncle Albert (b) Brede (c) Brian Rafferty and (d) Mr Blake.

4 Describe three scenes of violence in the novel, bringing out clearly the atmosphere created by the author and the dramatic nature of the incident.

5 Write about any single incident in the book (in some detail) which you found either romantic or exciting or humorous.

6 Imagine that you are one of the boys who helped Brian Rafferty to beat up Kevin. Make an entry in your diary to say exactly what happened, why you took part, and what your feelings are now that it is over.

7 Imagine that you are the soldier who found the gun. Write down in question and answer form your interrogation of Kate Kelly when she came to make her statement incriminating Kevin. Say afterwards what made you doubtful about the truth of what she said.

8 Write a letter from Sadie to her parents saying why she had decided to join Kevin and leave Ireland. You should refer to events in the book which may have influenced Sadie in her decision.

9 Read the last two chapters of the novel carefully. When you have done this, write a piece of coursework saying whether you think the ending is satisfactory or not. You must base your answer on the events of the story and their effects on the different characters who play their parts in it.

10 From your reading of *Across the Barricades* say what you have learned of the conflict in Ireland in terms of (a) the facts and (b) the reactions of individuals and groups. You should refer closely to the novel in your answer.

Adolescence and love

Some of the novels you will be studying will be about adolescence, dealing with people in your own age-group or close to it, or they may even explore the nature of younger children. *Gregory's Girl*, which was originally a play for television, is a well-written story about the life and fantasies of a sixteen-year-old boy. He is in a school football team which loses all its matches until a girl attends one of the trials and, despite the bewilderment and the objections of the games master, gets her place in the team as a striker. They cease to lose, she becomes the centre of attraction and publicity, the Headmaster approves her selection, and Gregory falls in love with her, or thinks he falls in love with her. What he really wants is a girl-friend, and by the end of the story he has one, though it is not the girl-footballer he coveted. This novel by Gerald Cole, which is in the Collins Cascades series, is enjoyable and stimulating reading. The language is vivid, racy, colloquial; the dialogue natural and unforced. There is plenty of humour and incident and you'll enjoy reading it.

Assignments

Write on one or more of the following:

1 Describe Gregory's reactions to Dorothy, and give an account of how his life is dominated by her right up to the date that he finally thinks he has got with her.

2 Gregory often fantasizes. Describe any two of his fantasies, and then write about any fantasy you have had which bears some resemblance to Gregory's.

3 Which incident in the novel do you find the most humorous and why?

Notes

Introduction Gregory's 'date' with Dorothy – Gregory's wait at the terminus – the coat – too large – its effect – more suited to the ballroom – Gregory's thoughts/plans for Dorothy – 'the problem of the noses' – passage of time – Gregory frantic – more rehearsing of what he will do – adjustment of smile – THEN

Para 2 Carol not Dorothy – effect on Gregory – her news re Dorothy – Gregory's 'halting, tuneless whistle' – denial (and lie) over the coat – Gregory's thoughts about not wasting the date – the walk to the chip-shop – Carol using him – the telephone-box incident – his fear of public embarrassment – the transformation of Carol – Gregory's shyness and fear as a result – bring out humour of Carol's appearance and her manhandling Gregory down the street – has to go with this 'punk monstrosity' and in front of people who know him too – Gregory's verbal humour at the expense of Ricky Swift – THEN

Para 3 Write a paragraph on the humour in the Margo episode (selective points as above) THEN

Conclusion Susan – the humour of the interchanges between Gregory and her (indicate the nature of this) – bring out clearly the fact that all this is arranged, so that in the end we laugh (a) at Gregory being duped (b) with Gregory at himself and (c) at the sheer pace and enjoyment of the episode.

4 Give an account of life in the school as it is presented to us, bringing out the relationships between members of staff and staff and pupils.

5 Write character sketches of Phil Menzies and Steve, bringing out clearly their obsessions with football and cookery respectively.

6 Imagine that you are Dorothy, and that you discuss with your friends, 'gaol-bait 5A', the idea of attending the football trial. Tell them about your experiences in the trial and describe as vividly as you can the first game that you played for Climackton Comprehensive. You may write this in the form of a dialogue with Carol, Margo and Susan if you wish.

7 Write about the scene or incident in the novel which you enjoyed most.

8 Compare Gregory and his attitudes and experiences with any other story in which a boy is the central character. You might consider, for example, J. D. Salinger's *The Catcher in the Rye* (Penguin Books) where the narrator Holden Caulfield (somewhat older than Gregory, though not that much) drops out of college, dates a girl, then a prostitute, and knows that he has one real friend in the world, his little sister 'Old Phoebe'.

If you have not read Gregory's Girl *but have studied another novel or short story which deals with adolescence, adapt some of the assignments to fit your book.* Write about character, atmosphere, excitement or tension or humour, sadness, the unusual or unexpected, or particular incidents or situations. Then develop some aspect of the book which shows that you can write imaginatively about what you have read, for example, bearing in mind what the adolescent character is like, write an account of his early adult life as it might be – job, leisure, marriage, happenings etc.

It is not possible, in a book of this nature, to encompass a wide range of texts and indicate in each case what the main themes of the various books are. But the books you are studying will have themes, and often these provide a way of exploring the text in some detail and of getting to know the author's intentions. Some themes do not admit of a single-word definition, some do. We might consider that the main theme of *Jane Eyre* is the spirited independence of the heroine, and an appraisal of Jane's character and reactions throughout the novel would support this. If you are studying the book, consider Jane's reactions to Mrs Reed and the bullying ways of John Reed: examine her relationship with Helen Burns and her going to Helen on the night of the latter's death. Consider how at various crisis points in her life Jane displays her independence (indeed one of the great achievements of this novel is the consistent way in which the main character is presented). Her independence can be seen when she decides to leave Lowood, when she refuses to become Rochester's mistress and also in her rejection of St John Rivers. The interested reader will find a number of lesser instances, and will perhaps be able to link this theme to others which are part of the novel's texture, for example truthfulness, conscience, practical as distinct from theoretical christianity, superficiality (Blanche Ingram and her entourage and Adèle), hypocrisy, duty. It would be possible to enlarge upon this. The point is that you should search out the theme or themes in the book you are reading. They will help you to understand the characters the author has created, and perhaps the attitudes or intentions of the author himself.

In the course of this book we have had occasion to look at Harper Lee's *To Kill a Mockingbird*, and no apology is needed for including an extract from it here. The theme of the novel, as has been indicated, is a pro-humanitarian anti-racist one and, despite the fact that it was published in 1960 and is set back in time to the period 1933–5, it is particularly relevant to our own time when prejudice of an irrational nature often produces extreme situations, tensions which lead to violence. We must emphasize that no theme exists in isolation, and the extract below, while it underlines by its very situation the themes of the novel, also provides vital material for analysis, comment, interpretation and imaginative writing.

> '. . . Robert E. Lee Ewell!'
> In answer to the clerk's booming voice, a little bantam cock of a man rose and strutted to the stand, the back of his neck reddening at the sound of his name. When he turned around to take the oath, we saw that his face was red as his neck. We also saw no resemblance to his namesake. A shock of wispy new-washed hair stood up from his forehead; his nose was thin, pointed, and shiny; he had no chin to speak of – it seemed to be a part of his crepey neck.
> '– so help me God,' he crowed.
> Every town the size of Maycomb had families like the Ewells. No economic fluctuations changed their status – people like the Ewells lived as guests of the county in prosperity as well as in the depths of a depression. No truant officers could keep their numerous offspring in school; no public health officer could free them from congenital defects, various worms, and the diseases indigenous to filthy surroundings.
> Maycomb's Ewells lived behind the town garbage dump in what was once a Negro cabin.

> (Chapter 17)

This description comes in the first of three chapters devoted to the trial of Tom Robinson. Read the above extract carefully, and then test your understanding of it by answering the following questions (you may need to refer to a dictionary or the *Encyclopedia Britannica*).

1 Is Bob Ewell a likeable character or not? Give reasons for your answer – quote from the extract if necessary.

2 Who was Robert E. Lee? Why do you think that Ewell was named after him? (Remember where this novel is set and what the background to it is.)

3 What is meant by the words 'crepey' and 'indigenous'?

4 Explain the meaning of the following phrases: 'economic fluctuations' and 'congenital defects'.

5 What does the author mean by 'the Ewells lived as guests of the county'?

6 This is the beginning of the trial of the negro Tom Robinson for the rape of Mayella Ewell, Bob Ewell's daughter. Bearing that in mind, comment on what the author is saying in the last sentence of the extract.

Assignments

1 Imagine that you are Bob Ewell. Write an account of your journey to the court that day, saying what was going through your mind on the journey. Describe the court as you entered it, noting the presence of friends, relations etc. Rehearse your testimony while you wait, and describe your feelings as you take your stand in the witness-box.

2 Imagine that you are a reporter from a neighbouring town. Write an account for your newspaper of the proceedings in court. (You will need to read Chapters 17–21 of *To Kill a Mockingbird* to get the full atmosphere of the trial.) Your editor has allowed you 600 words, plus a main headline and a secondary one. Keep to these words limits, set your work out as if it were a newspaper column, and make your account as vivid and immediate as you can. Remember that the newspaper owner wants to sell copies, that your editor is hard-pressed and cannot give much time to revising your work. Remember also that the town you come from is influenced by the same attitudes as the people in Maycomb.

3 Imagine that you are Tom Robinson. Bearing in mind what has happened before the trial and the accusations made against you, write a letter to your mother describing events from your arrest to the first day of the trial.

Notes

You might refer to your own home, how the police or the sheriff came to it, your bewilderment at the charge, your memory of casual conversations with Mayella, your feeling sorry for her. Then you could go on to your despair in gaol, the comfort you receive from knowing that Atticus Finch is to defend you, your fears when you hear there is a lynch-mob after you. End the letter about half-an hour before you are taken into court, and describe what you are feeling at this time. Your mother lives some 200 miles away, and by the time she gets the letter, the trial will be over and you will know the worst.

Style

In any piece of coursework you undertake it is necessary for you to respond to the language used by the writer. The word 'style' at the head of this extract has formal connotations for many people, but here we mean the distinctive usages of individual writers as well as the general term to describe the language, whether dialogue, imagery, description for example, which they use. It is through the medium of language that the author presents character, creates setting, reveals or comments on behaviour, or employs imagery with a particular emphasis. It has already been noted how effectively Charlotte Brontë describes the background to Rochester's proposal to Jane. Her language conveys all the lush warmth of a balmy midsummer's evening, helping to create the appropriate background for the super-charged atmosphere which characterises the whole scene. In the following extract from D. H. Lawrence's short story 'Odour of Chrysanthemums' we note the various ways in which the author brings home to the reader the awesome sadness and finality of death. Read it slowly and carefully in order to get its full flavour, looking particularly at the various uses of language which it employs:

'I must wash him,' she said.

Then the old mother rose stiffly, and watched Elizabeth as she carefully washed his face, carefully brushing the big blond moustache from his mouth with the flannel. She was afraid with a bottomless fear, so she ministered to him. The old woman, jealous, said:

'Let me wipe him!' – and she kneeled on the other side drying slowly as Elizabeth washed, her big black bonnet sometimes brushing the dark head of her daughter-in-law. They worked thus in silence for a long time. They never forgot it was death, and the touch of the man's dead body gave them strange emotions, different in each of the women; a great dread possessed them both, the mother felt the lie was given to her womb, she was denied; the wife felt the utter isolation of the human soul, the child within her was a weight apart from her.

At last it was finished. He was a man of handsome body, and his face showed no traces of drink. He was blond, full-fleshed, with fine limbs. But he was dead.

'Bless him,' whispered his mother, looking always at his face, and speaking out of sheer terror. 'Dear lad – bless him!' She spoke in a faint, sibilant ecstasy of fear and mother love.

Elizabeth sank down again to the floor, and put her face against his neck, and trembled and shuddered. But she had to draw away again. He was dead, and her living flesh had no place against his. A great dread and weariness held her: she was so unavailing. Her life was gone like this.

You will note how effectively and economically Lawrence employs dialogue, description and reveals character through particular emphases. The awe and unease of the occasion are felt in the tense dialogue, which seems to punctuate the silence and care with which the women work. You notice words like 'faint' and 'whispered' and that the old mother seems to be talking to herself, perhaps remembering the dead miner as a child. The language is clear. There is an unerring feeling for the right word in the right context. The sombre atmosphere is intensified by the way in which the women work in silence with the emphasis on 'death', 'strange emotions', 'fear' and 'dread'. Notice the references to 'the big black bonnet', the 'dark head' and the 'utter isolation of the human soul' which convey a special funereal dread of their own. The dead man is no longer a creature of warmth and sunlight; the deathly cold of his skin makes his wife shudder. The shattering finality of death is emphasized in the words: 'He was blond, full fleshed, with fine limbs. But he was dead.' The staccato rhythm of the words seems to echo the tense conversation of the two women.

This is a fraught and moving scene, and part of its effectiveness is seen in the interaction between wife and mother-in-law. Notice the balance of 'wash' and 'wipe', the fact that the mother is jealous and wants her share of her son, even in death. Particularly poignant is the contrast, the deliberate emphasis on birth and death as it affects each of them. The mother feels 'the lie was given to her womb, she was denied', in other words, what she produced at birth all those years ago is now dead, her child is dead. Lawrence here employs contrast very effectively, since Elizabeth, who is carrying her dead husband's child, feels the separation of what has happened. She and her dead husband can no longer be one flesh, so 'the child within her was a weight apart from her'. Here the intensity in the use of language is marked, with an emphasis too on the fact that Elizabeth will have to bear the child – and the economic burden of bearing the child – alone. Her isolation is already evident. The last paragraph of the extract focuses upon her, and again we note the cunning use of language, 'Her life was gone like this'. The immediacy of death gives Elizabeth the illusion of being dead herself or, more accurately perhaps, of living on in a kind of dead life.

Assignments

Elizabeth has been waiting for some time for her husband to return home from the pit where he works. She has been with her children during this time, but they have been sent to bed. Elizabeth feels that her husband has gone to the public house on his way home, and spent the evening there drinking, as he often does this. She is wrong. There has been an accident at the pit, and he is brought home dead. This is where the extract given above begins. Write on one of the following:

1 Imagine that you are Elizabeth. Write a letter to your own mother, explaining what has happened and saying what your plans for the future are (you can go into detail about funeral arrangements, children etc).

2 Imagine that you are one of the children upstairs. You lie awake thinking, wondering why your father has not come home. Write down your thoughts as you lie in bed right up to the point when you hear someone entering the house. You may include any references to your father, mother, or day-to-day events in your thoughts.

3 Imagine you are the mother in this extract. Next day you are comforted by a neighbour. Explain what happened during the evening, from the time you called at your daughter-in-law's house right through until you left after tending the body of your son. You should refer to the extract given above, but you can 'invent' in order to make the account to the neighbour ring true. Naturally, some of the neighbour's words may come into your writing.

4 Write about any moment of crisis in your life, and try to use words which convey what you felt. Do not use clichés (expressions which have become stale and therefore meaningless) and do not use too much dialogue.

Dialogue

The writing of dialogue is an important aspect of the writer's technique. Much of the story will appear more immediate and more vital if it can be incorporated into the dialogue. Too much descriptive writing may create the impression that the reader is not intimately concerned with the fortunes of the characters and the progress of events. The successful use of dialogue can help to create the exciting impression that the reader is actually witnessing the events taking place.

In the following extract, Gabriel Oak meets a timid and unnamed girl on the road to Weatherbury in Hardy's *Far From The Madding Crowd*:

> She extended her hand; Gabriel his. In feeling for each other's palm in the gloom before the money could be passed, a minute incident occurred which told much. Gabriel's fingers alighted on the young woman's wrists. It was beating with a throb of tragic intensity. He had frequently felt the same quick, hard beat in the femoral artery of his lambs when overdriven. It suggested a consumption too great of a vitality which, to judge from her figure and stature, was already too little.
>
> 'What is the matter?'
>
> 'Nothing.'
>
> 'But there is?'
>
> 'No, no, no! Let your having seen me be a secret!'
>
> 'Very well; I will. Good-night, again.'
>
> 'Good-night.'
>
> The young girl remained motionless by the tree, and Gabriel descended into the village of Weatherbury, or Lower Longpuddle as it was sometimes called. He fancied that he had felt himself in the penumbra of a very deep sadness when touching that slight and fragile creature. But wisdom lies in moderating mere impressions, and Gabriel endeavoured to think little of this.

This brief, hurried conversation in the dark conveys an air of mystery and suspense. What is the unnamed girl's secret? Why doesn't she want it revealed? Why is she going to Weatherbury? This piece of dialogue makes the story more immediate and more vital and lays clues for the reader which will be essential in understanding the plot. Hardy makes us feel as if we are actually witnessing the meeting.

Dialogue should be: interesting – it must help to maintain the interest of the reader – and appropriate – it should fit the character who is speaking. The language should be suggestive – in an exciting or mysterious situation the dialogue should reflect this. In the above brief conversation there is, for example, both distinct tension and excitement.

Dialogue of course rarely exists in any extended sequence on its own. Frequently it is combined with description or commentary; it must strike just the right note if the sequence is dramatic or exciting. Dialogue is the natural expression of dramatic tension, the outward expression of what the character feels within at the precise moment of tension.

In the following extract, you will be able to consider exactly how the author uses dialogue, description and inward monologue to achieve a sequence of high drama, in which the unexpected, the sudden danger, the reactions and actions all combine to produce a strong effect on the reader. More than that, the atmosphere and the happenings have a sense of mystery about them too. The reader familiar with *Jane Eyre* will note Jane's reference to Grace Poole, whom she believes to be the possessor of the demoniac laugh which she hears from time to time in the upper reaches of Thornfield. The other names mentioned are those of servants and Mrs Fairfax is the housekeeper. If you are not familiar with the novel, read the extract for its dramatic quality, both in description and dialogue, and look at the questions set below. You may be able to use or adapt some of them to a particular book you are studying in which there is a dangerous incident:

> Something creaked: it was a door ajar, and that door was Mr Rochester's, and the smoke rushed in a cloud from thence. I thought no more of Mrs Fairfax; I thought no more of Grace Poole or the laugh: in an instant, I was within the chamber. Tongues of flame darted round the bed: the curtains were on fire. In the midst of blaze and vapour, Mr Rochester lay stretched motionless, in deep sleep.
>
> 'Wake! wake!' I cried – I shook him, but he only murmured and turned: the smoke had stupefied him. Not a moment could be lost: the very sheets were kindling. I rushed to his basin and ewer; fortunately, one was wide and the other deep, and both were filled with water. I heaved them up, deluged the bed and its occupant, flew back to my own room, brought my own water-jug, baptized the couch afresh, and, by God's aid, succeeded in extinguishing the flames which were devouring it.
>
> The hiss of the quenched element, the breakage of a pitcher which I had flung from my hand when I had emptied it, and, above all, the splash of the shower-bath I had liberally bestowed, roused Mr Rochester at last. Though it was now dark, I knew he was awake; because I heard him fulminating strange anathemas at finding himself lying in a pool of water.
>
> 'Is there a flood?' he cried.
>
> 'No, sir,' I answered; 'but there has been a fire: get up, do, you are quenched now; I will fetch you a candle'.
>
> 'In the name of all the elves in Christendom, is that Jane Eyre?' he demanded. 'What had you done with me, witch, sorceress? Who is in the room besides you? Have you plotted to drown me?'
>
> 'I will fetch you a candle, sir; and, in Heaven's name, get up. Somebody has plotted something: you cannot too soon find out who and what it is'.
>
> 'There – I am up now; but at your peril you fetch a candle yet: wait two minutes till I get into some dry garments, if any dry there be – yes, here is my dressing-gown. Now run!'

I did run; I brought the candle which still remained in the gallery. He took it from my hand, held it up, and surveyed the bed, all blackened and scorched, the sheets drenched, the carpet round swimming in water.

'What is it? and who did it?' he asked.

I briefly related to him what had transpired: the strange laugh I had heard in the gallery; the step ascending to the third storey; the smoke, – the smell of fire which had conducted me to his room; in what state I had found matters there, and how I had deluged him with all the water I could lay hands on.

He listened very gravely; his face, as I went on, expressed more concern than astonishment; he did not immediately speak when I had concluded.

'Shall I call Mrs Fairfax?' I asked.

'Mrs Fairfax? No: what the deuce would you call her for? What can she do? Let her sleep unmolested.'

'Then I will fetch Leah, and wake John and his wife.'

'Not at all: just be still. You have a shawl on? If you are not warm enough, you may take my cloak yonder; wrap it about you, and sit down in the arm-chair: there, – I will put it on. Now place your feet on the stool, to keep them out of the wet. I am going to leave you a few minutes. I shall take the candle. Remain where you are till I return; be as still as a mouse. I must pay a visit to the second storey. Don't move, remember, or call any one'.

1 What do you learn of Jane from this extract?

2 How does the author set about establishing an atmosphere of excitement *and* mystery. Refer to the text and choose phrases which contribute to the effect of the extract.

3 What do you learn of Mr Rochester in this extract?

4 Concentrate on the dialogue in this extract: do you find it natural and, if so, why? What does it contribute to our understanding and appreciation of the incident?

5 Consider the language that is not given in the form of speech. Indicate which you think is the most important, that used to describe Jane's thoughts and reactions, or that which is used to describe the physical elements of this scene?

6 Study the last paragraph of the extract closely. What does the language tell you of Rochester's state of mind? Bearing in mind what you know of the story, what do you think he is going to do and why? You should refer to the plot in your answer.

7 Give an account of a dramatic or critical incident from your own experience in which you, or someone you know, had to display considerable presence of mind in dealing with the situation.

Descriptive language and imagery

You should refer back to the extract from *Of Mice and Men* on p. 44 of this book. There you will find descriptive language (specifically of nature) and images (metaphors and similes, for example) which enrich the language and make it the more vivid or vital to the reader. Similes, introduced by *like* or *as*, frequently stimulate the reader to think about the basis of the comparison. In one novel a motorway is seen as being 'like a blue ribbon of cigarette smoke'. It is an apt comparison, since it conveys the viewer's distance, perspective from it. In Barry Hines' *Kes* Jud is described as being 'like a man in fetters', another appropriate simile, since he is, at the time, drunk, in other words a prisoner of drink. Metaphors are built-in comparisons without using like or as. In the same sequence from *Kes* Jud has a 'blind smile', while much later in the novel Billy pulls 'a sucked lemon face' and also stands 'stork fashion', that is, on one leg.

Description covers a whole range of subjects – nature, buildings, interiors etc, and has already been dealt with under *Setting*. But description of people is an important index to personality, and in nineteenth-century fiction it is normally the prelude to the deeper psychological investigation which accompanies character in action. Look at Hardy's description of Gabriel Oak at the beginning of *Far From the Madding Crowd*:

> When Farmer Oak smiled, the corners of his mouth spread till they were within an unimportant distance of his ears, his eyes were reduced to chinks, and diverging wrinkles appeared round them, extending upon his countenance like the rays in a rudimentary sketch of the rising sun.

It is a vivid piece of description, enhanced by the image in the last line, and blends appearance and character so that we get the impression of a person rather than a stereotyped drawing.

Dickens too is good at emphasizing particular traits which make the person larger than life. In *A Tale of Two Cities* Mr Lorry is described in some detail in Chapter 4. He has a good leg, 'an odd little sleek crisp flaxen wig' and 'A face habitually suppressed and quieted, was still lighted up under the quaint wig by a pair of moist bright eyes'

. . . He had a healthy colour in his cheeks, and his face, though lined, bore few traces of anxiety'. The visual quality which Dickens brings to bear here is common in his work, allied to an individual imaginative quality which personalizes places as well as people, as in this same chapter where he writes that 'The little, narrow, crooked town of Dover hid itself away from the beach, and ran its head into the chalk cliffs, like a marine ostrich. The beach was a desert of heaps of sea and stones tumbling wildly about, and the sea did what it liked, and what it liked was destruction.' When you read descriptions like that, look at the nature of the language and define how it affects your own response.

Now that you have considered the various aspects of fiction covered here from 'Plot' onwards, read the following passage from Orwell's *Animal Farm* and undertake the assignments, both of interpretation and imaginative expansion, which are listed below:

Silent and terrified, the animals crept back into the barn. In a moment the dogs came bounding back. At first no one had been able to imagine where these creatures came from, but the problem was soon solved: they were the puppies whom Napoleon had taken away from their mothers and reared privately. Though not yet full-grown, they were huge dogs, and as fierce-looking as wolves. They kept close to Napoleon. It was noticed that they wagged their tails to him in the same way as the other dogs had been used to do to Mr Jones.

Napoleon, with the dogs following him, now mounted on the raised portion of the floor where Major had previously stood to deliver his speech. He announced that from now on the Sunday morning Meetings would come to an end. They were unnecessary, he said, and wasted time. In future all questions relating to the working of the farm would be settled by a special committee of pigs, presided over by himself. These would meet in private and afterwards communicate their decisions to the others. The animals would still assemble on Sunday mornings to salute the flag, sing 'Beasts of England', and receive their orders for the week; but there would be no more debates.

In spite of the shock that Snowball's expulsion had given them, the animals were dismayed by this announcement. Several of them would have protested if they could have found the right arguments. Even Boxer was vaguely troubled. He set his ears back, shook his forelock several times and tried hard to marshal his thoughts; but in the end he could not think of anything to say. Some of the pigs themselves, however, were more articulate. Four young porkers in the front row uttered shrill squeals of disapproval, and all four of them sprang to their feet and began speaking at once. But suddenly the dogs sitting round Napoleon let out deep, menacing growls, and the pigs fell silent and sat down again. Then the sheep broke out into a tremendous bleating of 'Four legs good, two legs bad!' which went on for nearly a quarter of an hour and put an end to any chance of discussion.

Afterwards Squealer was sent round the farm to explain the new arrangements to the others.

'Comrades', he said, 'I trust that every animal here appreciates the sacrifice that Comrade Napoleon has made in taking this extra labour upon himself. Do not imagine, comrade, that leadership is a pleasure! On the contrary, it is a deep and heavy responsibility. No one believes more firmly than Comrade Napoleon that all animals are equal. He would be only too happy to let you make your decisions for yourselves. But sometimes you might make the wrong decisions, comrades, and then where should we be? Suppose you had decided to follow Snowball, with his moonshine of windmills – Snowball, who, as we now know, was no better than a criminal?'

1 The setting is the barn. How important is this in considering the impact made by this particular scene upon the reader? You should refer to the extract in your answer.

2 Compare and contrast the effect achieved by *reporting* the words of Napoleon and giving the actual speech of Squealer. Why do you think the author does this?

3 Identify the main theme or themes in this extract, quoting from the text or referring to it to illustrate the points you are making.

4 Imagine you are a member of this audience. Write a letter to a friend saying what caused the meeting and describing the reactions at it. You should use this extract as the basis for your answer, but you may include any reactions (whispers, mutters etc) which you observed at the time.

5 There are a number of statements which curtail the freedom of the animals. Quote these, and say how seriously you regard them.

6 *Animal Farm* is George Orwell's fable dealing with extremism and dictatorship. Point out the *human* qualities shown by the animals here and say whether you find them convincing or not.

7 Write an account of any meeting that you have attended in which there were areas of disagreement among the audience and/or the speakers. You may use dialogue or reported speech or both in your answer.

Short stories

All examinations boards will offer you selections of short stories to study. These are usually of three kinds. A collection of stories on a particular theme, for example 'Science Fiction' or 'Childhood'; a collection of short stories by different authors linked together by their ideas or themes or by their setting; a collection of stories by one writer e.g. D. H. Lawrence or Bill Naughton.

It is important that you should know what happens in each story and be prepared to discuss the author's ideas and attitudes as well as his characters and setting. You should also be ready to identify the common features of stories written by one author or similarities between stories written by different writers.

The setting

In short stories the setting is very important and may be even more crucial than the plot. Setting may be in a special time, such as Ray Bradbury's 'To Sing Strange Songs', or John Wyndham's 'The Seeds of Time', both of which are set in the future. Some may be set in a particular geographical location, such as Thomas Hardy's Wessex of the early nineteenth century. Stories which are set in local surroundings are often full of interesting detail and many of these, for instance Stan Barstow's short stories, reflect the author's personal background.

When writing coursework assignments based on the short story, remember the importance of planning, mentioned earlier.

How to tackle a short story

Read the story right through in one sitting. This will be a brief introduction. Try to visualize the setting, the central characters and the major elements of the plot. If there are any questions printed in the notes at the end of your story, study these. They may give you some indication of important points you should be looking out for. You should then read the story again and make detailed notes. Concentrate on the following: (a) how the story begins; (b) what gives the story its basic tension or conflict or humour or any other special quality; (c) the incidents, the complications, the climax, the resolution, the conclusion, with particular emphasis on a twist if there is one (d) the traits of the main characters (e) how is the story written? Does the writer arouse interest quickly, how does he/she establish a mood? Or secure suspense? Is there an economy of style?

If you were asked to look at Graham Greene's short story 'The Destructors' from *Twentieth-Century Short Stories* edited by D. R. Barnes and R. F. Egford, a selection used by many schools, this is the way you might organize your notes.

1 *How does the story develop?* It begins with Trevor, or T as he is known, visiting the house of Old Misery. He tells the others that it is a beautiful house, built by Sir Christopher Wren, with a wonderful staircase and panelling two hundred years old. He tells them Old Misery is going away on holiday and proposes that the gang should destroy the whole house.

2 *Basic conflict* An unlikely, strange, imperturbable boy joins the Wormsley Common Gang – by sheer force of personality he is accepted – in spite of the fact that he is called Trevor and his father is an architect who has come down in the world, the others do not make fun of him, and soon he supplants Blackie as the leader of the gang. By this exertion of personality T persuades the other members of the gang to participate in a monstrous act of vandalism.

3 *The climax and resolution of the story* The gang set to work and destroy everything in the house. T even burns Old Misery's savings. He declares he feels neither love nor hate for the man whose property he is destroying.

Suspense As the gang are destroying the walls of the house they hear the news that Old Misery is returning earlier than expected. The gang trick him into a W.C. and he is locked in. Next morning a lorry driver starts his lorry and as he drives forward, the remains of the house come crashing down.

4 *Traits of the main character* Powers lie in his complete concentration – single-mindedness – he has greater knowledge of building structure because his father is an architect – no sense of humour – takes himself very seriously – nothing diverts him from his purpose – T regards human emotions as 'soft'.

5 *Setting and style* Rather seedy and sordid – set in a house damaged during the war – children amusing themselves among half-shattered buildings. Latent violence in the story – T uses the primitive destructive instincts of the boys to deprive a pathetic old man of his home.

True to life The author develops both character and incident through dialogue. All the boys are real people and act from motives which most boys would understand.

Once you have read Graham Greene's story thoroughly and made detailed notes you would be in a position to plan your coursework assignment.

Assignment

> As a reporter for your local newspaper you are asked to cover the case of T and his gang at your local magistrate's court. Try and penetrate the strange mask of this imperturbable boy and account for his behaviour.

Notes

A detailed plan of your assignment might look like this:

Introduction Over a period of three days a listed house – believed to have been designed by Sir Christopher Wren – completely destroyed by a gang of vandals – leader of vandals in court – local architect's son – no remorse for the deed – member of a group known as Wormsley Common Gang – frequented derelict and bombed buildings.

Para 2 Factual account of the events as they are related to the court – gang leader decides to destroy property of Mr Thomas, an elderly man, over August Bank Holiday while owner is on holiday. House broken into and systematically smashed to pieces – serious damage done to walls and roof – old man returns early from his holiday and is locked in a W.C. – lorry driver pulls down house inadvertently as he drives away by a rope which has been attached to the back of his lorry.

Para 3 Magistrates appalled at the magnitude and seriousness of this act of wanton destruction – some attempt made to discover gang leader's motive – gang leader claims he neither loves nor hates house owner – gang leader not a thief – admits he burnt Mr Thomas's savings – police unable to determine the gang's motive.

Para 4   Report of child psychologist on leader of gang – boy from very secure family background – strong personality – no sense of humour – takes everything very seriously – determined to do everything as thoroughly as possible – held in respect and some awe by other members of the gang.

Conclusion   Effect on house owner – taken to local hospital suffering from shock – Parents very upset and disturbed. Local youth leader offers explanation – Gang leader was small, ineffective boy who wished to impress gang – used his organizational ability and technical knowledge to make himself leader.

Once you have drawn up a detailed plan of your assignment you can begin to write.

Further assignments

1 Imagine that you are the magistrate hearing the case. Make notes on the trial of the boys, bringing out clearly your attitude to T and to the other boys involved. What kind of punishment for them would you consider and why?

2 You are T's father. Write a letter to the magistrate saying what kind of boy he is at home etc, and giving examples of the good side of his character. Try to explain to the magistrate why you think T is as he is.

3 Imagine that you are Old Misery (Mr Thomas). Describe events from the time that you arrived back in your vandalized home and what your feelings were when you realized exactly what had happened. You may, if you like, write this as if it were the evidence at the magistrate's court.

Studying the short stories of one author

The short stories of Thomas Hardy are set in one particular geographical location, the area of Wessex, made up of the county of Dorset and its surrounding areas. Hardy was particularly interested in folklore and the way of life of the Dorset country folk, and looking at his stories you should be aware of the way in which he uses plot (with unexpected twists), descriptions (to create the superb settings for his stories) and dialogue (to create a realistic setting for the action).

In his short story 'The Withered Arm' Hardy starts by creating a superbly authentic scene as a troop of 'milkers' get to work on a dairy farm – 'The time of year was as yet early April, the feed lay entirely in water-meadows, and the cows were in "full pail".' The sound of a voice interrupts the flow of narrative – 'He do bring home his bride to-morrow, I hear.' With the first piece of dialogue the author links us to the central conflict of the story. Not only does the rustic dialect add to the country setting but it is actually used as a vehicle for conveying the plot.

In 'The Withered Arm' one of the central characters, Gertrude, suffers from a strange and mysterous wasting disease, starting from a place on the arm, shaped like a hand-print. She is told that this may be cured by touching the neck of a recently hanged man. Notice Hardy's economy of language and creation of atmosphere in the following almost furtive and breathless meeting between Gertrude and the executioner:

> 'You should really have gone to the governor of the jail, and your doctor with 'ee, and given your name and address – that's how it used to be done, if I recollect. Still perhaps, I can manage it for a trifling fee.'
> 'O, thank you! I would rather do it this way, as I should like it kept private.'
> 'Lover not to know, eh?'
> 'No – husband.'
> 'Aha! Very well. I'll get 'ee a touch of the corpse.'
> 'Where is it now?' she said, shuddering.
> 'It? – he, you mean; he's living yet. Just inside that little small winder up there in the glum.'

Note how Hardy uses words tellingly but economically to create atmosphere – mystery – dread and how the use of local dialect gives the story colour, background and realism. The subject matter – the touching of a hanged criminal's neck – suggests that the story is set early in the nineteenth century (it was first published in 1888).

Further assignments

Conditions You are given one week's homework to read thoroughly and make detailed notes on 'The Withered Arm'. You are then asked to do one of the following pieces of work.

1 Write the script for a play about the gossip in the cowshed which would have resulted from one of the following:
(a) Rhoda's illegitimate child and her affair with Farmer Lodge.
(b) The strange and mysterious disease which Gertrude suffers from.
(c) Gertrude and Rhoda's visit to Conjurer Trendle.

2 Gertrude and Rhoda have kept secret diaries of the events related in 'The Withered Arm'. Taking extracts from these diaries show how each of them might have a different viewpoint of these occurrences.

The short story – development of the narrative

Some stories you read may contain little plot. Leave things in the air, and nothing may seem to have changed. After you have finished your reading, however, you may be left with a consciousness of viewing a particular situation differently, for instance in D. H. Lawrence's 'Odour of Chrysanthemums'. You may become aware of Elizabeth's sudden understanding that she has never really understood her husband, and that she is ashamed of her lack of perception.

A popular form of story is one that tells a tale recounting a series of events with a definite beginning, middle and end. Many skilled short story writers introduce sudden twists into the plot which create interest and a satisfying climax to the narrative. At the end of Hardy's 'The Withered Arm' Gertrude is able to touch the neck of a hanged man only to discover it is the illegitimate son of her husband Farmer Lodge.

In another of his short stories 'The Melancholy Hussar of the German Legion' Hardy skilfully draws the whole plot of the story to a dramatic and tragic climax. The heroine, Phyllis, is forced to make a snap decision which brings about the most devastating consequences.

In the story Phyllis is courted and won by the dissolute Humphrey Gould, who leaves soon afterwards for Bath. She later meets the romantic figure of Matthaus, a soldier in the German Legion. After a secret love affair, the pair plan to elope to Matthaus's home in Germany. As she is waiting at the crossroads to elope, Humphrey Gould suddenly returns with another man, and she is forced to alter her plans.

> More words in the same strain were casually dropped as the two men waited: words which revealed to her, as by a sudden illumination, the enormity of her conduct. The conversation was at length cut off by the arrival of the man with the vehicle. The luggage was placed in it, and they mounted, and were driven on in the direction from which she had just come.
>
> Phyllis was so conscience-stricken that she was at first inclined to follow them; but a moment's reflection led her to feel that it would only be bare justice to Matthaus to wait till he arrived, and explain candidly that she had changed her mind – difficult as the struggle would be when she stood face to face with him. She bitterly reproached herself for having believed reports which represented Humphrey Gould as false to his engagement, when, from what she now heard from his own lips, she gathered that he had been living full of trust in her. But she knew well enough who had won her love. Without him her life seemed a dreary prospect, yet the more she looked at his proposal the more she feared to accept it – so wild as it was, so vague, so venturesome. She had promised Humphrey Gould, and it was only his assumed faithlessness which had led her to treat that promise as nought. His solicitude in bringing her these gifts touched her; her promise must be kept, and esteem must take the place of love. She would preserve her self-respect. She would stay at home, and marry him, and suffer.
>
> Phyllis had thus braced herself to an exceptional fortitude when, a few minutes later, the outline of Matthaus Tina appeared behind a field-gate, over which he lightly leapt as she stepped forward. There was no evading it, he pressed her to his breast.
>
> 'It is the first and last time!' she wildly thought as she stood encircled by his arms.

Phyllis finally feels unable to go. Matthaus and his friend Christophe go ahead with their escape plan, but are caught in their attempt at desertion and executed. Another twist is revealed when we learn Humphrey Gould has only come back to let Phyllis know that he has married someone else!

As you read this story you should be aware of the clever way in which the plot is unravelled and the enormity of the tragic choice

Phyllis is forced to make. By doing what she thinks is good and honourable, she causes tragedy. Finally, try and enter into the story in an imaginative way yourself. How would you have acted if you were Phyllis?

Assignment

Write Matthaus's last letter to his mother before he is shot.

Notes

Introduction My dearest mother, how wretched I have felt since I have been in England. Do not understand the people or their language. Life in the army very hard – Very few friends outside the regiment. Have always felt homesick for Germany and the home of my youth.

Para 2 Met a lovely young English girl. Different from all the rest. Made me feel glad to be in England. Finally I decided to desert from my regiment, bringing Phyllis, my English girl, with me. We were to meet secretly and then travel to the coast. You were to come and pick us up in France!

Para 3 At the last minute she decided she could not come. Felt honour-bound to marry a man she was engaged to. What she did was for the best of reasons. It was because she was such a good person that she felt she could not go through with the elopement. Do not think too harshly of her. Know she still loves me. My feelings for her are very strong. Will be thinking about you and her at the end.

Para 4 Captured when the boat we had cut from its moorings took us to Jersey instead of France. Kept in prison for two months. Tried by court-martial and sentenced to death.

Conclusion No feelings of regret about what I have done. Only sorry to have caused my mother pain. End will be at the hands of my comrades and death will be swift. Will be thinking of my loved ones at the end.

In a piece of coursework of this nature it is important that you try and feel all the emotions and turmoil which Matthaus himself would have experienced. This is what will impart the *imaginative insight* which the examiner will be looking for. Now put yourself in the position of Phyllis and either (a) Write a defence of her actions from her point of view or, as indicated earlier (b) Write an account of what you think you would have done if you had been in her place.

As you study a short story your teacher may give you a number of assignments. Not every one may be suitable for submission to the examiners, but will be designed to give you a greater insight into the story. Coursework which involves diagrams, maps, family trees etc is useful and productive for you to undertake.

Further assignments

Some additional pieces of coursework on 'The Melancholy Hussar of the German Legion' which may help to develop your interest in the events might be:

1 Finding out the historical facts concerning the King's German Legion, a regiment which served the British government during the Napoleonic Wars.

2 Draw a sketch map of Matthaus's plan for escape.

3 Write the story of Humphrey Gould from his winning of Phyllis to his meeting and marrying another girl. You should include known facts about Humphrey in your answer.

Language assignments for GCSE based on the short story

At least one piece of coursework in the English Language examination will be based on something you have read. Indeed, all the examination boards will require you to respond to a variety of written texts, including whole works of fiction, prose, poetry and drama. The short story often lends itself to much creative work.

In 'The Vertical Ladder' by William Sansom, a young boy, Flegg, is dared to climb the rusty ladder of a giant gasometer. The author explores the boy's mind as he experiences panic, terror and isolation in his struggle to reach the top. Likewise, in Doris Lessing's short story 'Through the Tunnel', a young boy, Jerry, dares himself to do something both difficult and dangerous. He meets some French boys who have learned to swim through an underwater tunnel. Jerry decides to train himself to perform this feat and practises daily.

Although he experiences great physical danger and discomfort, such as nosebleeds, he finally achieves his ambition.

Here we have two stories based on events which could easily happen to any child. Everyone has done something dangerous at some time, which common sense dictates they should never have done. This, coupled with the terrifying fear of heights and enclosed spaces which most people dread, make both these stories chillingly realistic. You might be asked to do something like the following:

Assignment

Conditions You are given two weeks' of homework to read both short stories and make notes. In class, working in groups, you discuss how the authors manage to use language to create a feeling of suspense and terror. You are then given one week's homework to write the following assignment:

Everyone does something foolish and dangerous at some time during their life. Write an account of how you are dared to participate in a highly-reckless and terrifying event. This could be something which has really happened to you, or something which you have created from your own imagination.

For reasons given at the beginning of this section, short stories make an attractive choice for many students. We have indicated here certain approaches, and you should be able to follow these up by choosing stories with the approval of your teacher, or by having your teacher recommend stories which you can explore for yourself. You might choose three or four stories which have a related theme – childhood, happiness, conflict, violence, adventure etc. Because of the twist in some stories you may be able to concentrate on the use of the unexpected, the element of surprise which provides the narrative tension. The successful short story writer has to present character in action, sharply delineated, without the time to trace and explain psychological development. You should note this for, as we have observed, dialogue in stories is of major importance, since it is often the most economical way of showing character and situation at one and the same time.

Non-fiction

The purpose of autobiography has always been to reveal and comment upon the life of the person who himself is writing the book. The author, Gerald Durrell, in *My Family and Other Animals* begins by saying 'This is the story of a five-year sojourn that I and my family made on the Greek island of Corfu.' The book, however, is not so concerned with showing what was specifically individual about his own life as a child, but rather of showing his part in a communal life shared by his lively family. As he himself says:

> 'It,' the story, was originally intended to be a mildly nostalgic account of the natural history of the island, but I made a grave mistake by introducing my family into the book in the first few pages. Having got themselves on paper, they have proceeded to establish themselves and invite various friends to share the chapters. It was only with the greatest difficulty, and by exercising considerable cunning, that I managed to retain a few pages here and there which I could devote exclusively to animals.

In Laurie Lee's, *Cider With Rosie*, he too is more concerned with the continuity of village life and the present's link with the remote past, than with his own role in the events. Within the book he is less a character than a presence, recording the flavour of village happenings before the advent of modern development. When the young Lee does appear, the author makes him representative of the boys growing up in the Cotswolds at that particular time.

As a student you may well be asked to read a novel like *Cider With Rosie* or *My Family and Other Animals*. Your treatment of coursework assignments should not be substantially different to anything you may write on general fiction. There are, however, a few points which you should bear in mind.

As you start your detailed reading of the book you should consider and make notes on the following:

(a) *The writer's point of view* If the author's views are SUBJECTIVE it may be that he has a prejudiced or impartial view of events. In *Cider With Rosie* Laurie Lee appears to adopt a more OBJECTIVE view of the world. We see the village of Slade through his eyes, and, although his writing is sensitive and poetic, he does try to capture the flavour of village life both realistically and objectively. The reader is made aware of the boy Laurie doing his chores at home, his playing evening games like Fox and Hounds, his experiences in the village school, his membership in the church choir, his presence on village outings – all these aspects of his life are presented as perfectly ordinary.

(b) *The general details of the person's life* Make notes on Laurie's childhood experiences, his time at school, his neighbours and friends. When tackling a novel like this it might be a help if you construct a family tree of the 'Light' family. You will then be able to see Laurie's relationship to other members of his family, for instance his uncles, aunts and cousins.

(c) *Any outstanding traits of character the subject may have* Notice how as a writer, Laurie Lee never seems to individualize himself. All his private feelings seem to be submerged within the group and his own actions are rarely presented as being exceptional. You should be prepared to find reasons for this.

When you have read the book carefully and noted details about the subject's life and the point of view expressed by the writer, carefully reflect upon the book and consider the following:

1 *The nature and purpose of the work* Think about the writer's ideas and point of view. Is there any kind of theme? In *Cider With Rosie* Lee writes: 'I belonged to that generation which, saw, by chance, the end of a thousand years' life.' During the course of the book the author explores the nature of change and its effect upon the village. The idea behind the work may be that growing up in the early part of the twentieth century in a Cotswold village acquainted Laurie with a simple, traditional but enjoyable life, now for ever lost. Is Laurie Lee successful in presenting this picture?

2 *The accuracy and realism of the author's presentation* Laurie Lee is a poet and this is apparent in his style, especially in his descriptive passages. His descriptions of places, events and people are totally believable. Notice the way he describes his uncles. 'They were men of great strength, of bloody deeds, a fist of uncles arrived at the foe, riders of hell and apocalypse, each one half man, half horse.'

Not every piece of coursework will be of an open-ended, creative type. Some will be more traditional and test your awareness of some of the central issues in the book. The following example requires you to say something about the way in which the village of Slade loses its old feudal character and changes for ever.

Assignment

'I belonged to that generation which saw, by chance, the end of a thousand years' life. The change came late to our Cotswold valley, didn't really show itself till the late 1920's; I was twelve by then, but during that handful of years I witnessed the whole thing happen.' Discuss the way in which the village of Slade changes.

Notes

Introduction Time and change are important themes. Lee emphasizes time and again the continuity of village life, the present's link with the remote past. Villagers' superstitions are evidence of the beliefs of generations who had lived in the valley since the 'Stone Age'.

Para 2 Continuity by the use of older characters' memories. Old people of the village dress as their grandfathers did and speak in ancient dialect. Young girls called 'damsels', young boys 'squires', old men 'masters'. Villagers isolation caused by the horse: 'His eight miles an hour was the limit of our movements, as it had been since the days of the Romans'.

Para 3 Village's self-sufficient life, based on the land and the seasons, cannot resist the developments that take place in the wider world outside. Arrival of motor transport brings in the new age. Old people die of shock, faced by speeds they cannot understand.

Para 4 Slade now faces the influences of the outside world. The sun now no longer rises on their local hill, but it now rises in London in the east. Community which made its own amusements has gone. Now they are dependent on wireless.

Para 5 Beliefs and moral standards in the village now challenged. Church begins to lose its authority. Young people marry in registry offices. Laurie caught reading *Sons and Lovers*. The squire dies. Most important signs of his power – house and estate – are sold off. Servants take modern jobs in factories. As the old people die, their old ways of speech and dress die with them.

Conclusion   The death of the squire and the passing of the ancient way of life coincides with the break-up of Laurie's own family. As Laurie and his sisters leave home only their mother will be left to embody the values of older times.

As Kenneth Hardacre has rightly observed in his excellent study of *Cider With Rosie* (Brodie's Notes), 'It is a book which lies somewhere between autobiography and novel . . . *Cider With Rosie* is the story of a Gloucestershire childhood as seen by the adult that Laurie became: the incidents are determined by adult selection, coloured by adult impressions, and presented with all the conscious (and sometimes even self-conscious) artistry of an adult professional writer, who can heighten and tone down, exaggerate or underplay, as he wishes.' In a sense this places it very close (as Hardacre has noted) to James Joyce's *Portrait of the Artist as a Young Man*. We might note here that a novel much mentioned in this commentary, *To Kill a Mockingbird*, has points of contact with it too, since that *appears* to be Scout's auto-biography. When you are studying non-fiction you should use the same approaches as to fiction itself. Ask yourself, what makes this a book worth reading? What does it tell me about the writer and his interests? What particular qualities does this work have as literature? What episodes are outstanding and how am I affected by them? Are there scenes or situations or moods with which I can sympathize? Could I write appreciations of any of these and, because of the nature of the book, could I write imaginatively as a result of reading this book or aspects of it? The reader of Gavin Maxwell's superb book, *Ring of Bright Water*, can share the experiences and the enjoyment, and he/she can also find much to write about, whether in appreciation of Maxwell's style, his settings, particularly Camusfearna and its adja-cent bay, burn, waterfall, gorge, islands – all contribute, together with the account of the seasons, to the flavour of the book. But there are many other things which remain with the reader – the sense of isolation, the loneliness, the retreat, the haven. Each of these suggests an imaginative identification for the reader, just as the London scenes evoke a completely contrasting atmosphere. But *Ring of Bright Water* is mainly concerned with otters, and Mij and Edal, their routines, care, habits, relationships and characteristics. The joy and love in this focus are finely conveyed. The interested student can write about any number of things concerned with the individual otters. For example, one could examine the differences between Mij and Edal, or write an account of Mij's journeys or the language of otters. You could write on

Gavin Maxwell's experiences of other animals, for example, or you could examine the quality of his humour, his descriptive powers or what kind of a person he is judging from his dealings with animals and his observations on them.

Coursework based on controlled conditions

If your GCSE English Literature course is being assessed by 100% coursework you will almost certainly be asked to submit at least *one* piece of work which has been done under examination conditions. The material used for this will be provided by your teacher and will probably be based on one of the books that you have studied. Your teacher will not be able to help you with any part of this work and it must show your *own* spontaneous response to the text.

This work could be based on either a) a chapter of a novel b) a short story or c) an extract from non-fiction. It might also be based on a scene from a play or a poem and for guidance on how to tackle these particular literary forms we suggest that you consult the companion volume *English coursework: Drama and Poetry*.

What will this test consist of?

You could be asked to read a printed extract from one of your texts, and answer a number of questions which test your understanding of the piece. This would be the more formal way of conducting the examination and differs very little from the old CSE and GCE. Alternatively your teacher could use an open-book approach to the examination. You would be asked to either read a particular section and answer a number of questions which test your understanding of the passage or, read a chapter or section, and answer a few questions about the passage and *one* longer question which tests your knowledge of other areas of the text.

Assignments

The following assignment is based on E. R. Braithwaite's *To Sir with Love*. (E. R. Braithwaite was born in British Guyana. During the Second World War he fought with the RAF. He was a very well-qualified engineer, but was unable to find a job when the war ended because he was black. He was eventually offered a post in a tough East London school. At first he met a hostile reaction, but gradually he won the respect and affection of his pupils.)

Note The questions you answer on a text would fall into one of two categories, those which are designed to test your understanding of a passage and those which are more open-ended and ask for your opinion and personal response to all or part of it. As an example *two* of the former types of questions are shown and *one* of the latter.

Read Chapter 9 of *To Sir With Love* and answer the following questions:

1 Briefly summarize what Mr Braithwaite tells the class about the way he expects them to behave.

They must not interrupt. They should behave in a controlled, dignified manner. They should address him as Mr Braithwaite or sir. Girls will be referred to as 'miss', the boys by their surnames. Girls must show themselves worthy of respect. Boys are expected to be clean, with their shoes well brushed.

2 What reason does Mr Braithwaite give the class for expecting them to behave along the lines that he states?

In a short time they would be working for a living, and being polite and civil to others would be necessary for them. As we move from the state of childhood, certain higher standards of behaviour are expected from us.

3 Discuss what Mr Braithwaite says about smartness and toughness. Do you agree?

There is nothing weak or unmanly about clean hands and faces and shoes that are brushed. A man who is strong and tough never needs to show it in his dress or the way he cuts his hair. Toughness is a quality of the mind – nothing to do with muscles. *You are being asked for your opinion.* Whether you agree or disagree you *must* give your reasons.

A more challenging text may be Charles Dickens's *A Tale of Two Cities*. This is one of Dickens's most exciting novels set in Paris and London during the most violent period of the French Revolution.
Read Chapter 11 (Book 1) of *A Tale of Two Cities*.

1 How does Dickens convey the feeling of cold and discomfort suffered by the passengers?

Passengers had to walk uphill in the mire. Steaming mist in the hollows. Very cold – a clammy and intensely cold mist. Reek of the labouring horses. Passengers hidden under layers of wrappers. Constant fear of robbers – no-one wanted to communicate with anyone else – Guard has to stamp his feet because of the cold.

2 We get the feeling that something dangerous or mysterious could happen. How does Dickens convey this?

Danger is in the air. Guard suspected the passengers, passengers suspected one another and the guard, they all suspected everybody else – coachman sure of nothing but the horses. The warning voice of the coachman – Someone riding fast in the dark. Mysterious rider approaching at a gallop. Stillness of the night made it very quiet indeed. Panting of horses communicated a tremulous motion to the coach, as if in a state of agitation. The hearts of the passengers beat loud. People out of breath and holding their breath with expectation.

This last example from *A Tale of Two Cities* is designed to test your wider reading of the novel.

3 Select any other part of *A Tale of Two Cities* and show how Dickens conveys a sense of mystery or danger.

Notes

From Chapter 5, Book 1. Scene set near a wine shop in Saint Antoine in Paris. Cask of wine has been accidentally dropped in the street. In the street people have left their work to lap it up as it flows among the paving stones. To these people living amid appalling conditions of squalor, poverty and constant hunger, wine is like a blessing from Heaven. Sets the scene for the mysterious occurrences within the wine shop.

Mr Lorry and Miss Manette sit at a table. Monsieur Defarge chats to three mysterious men at the counter and there is a strange exchange of the Christian name 'Jacques' between them – sign of a secret association. As Mr Lorry and Lucy cross the foul-smelling courtyard and climb a staircase they meet the same mysterious, strange men outside Dr Manette's room – they are looking through a keyhole. Dr Manette a pitiful sight, faded and haggard. All he can do is mumble 'One Hundred and Five North Tower.' Dickens creates a sense of suspense and mystery. Who are the strange men called 'Jacques'? What is the relationship between Monsieur and Madame Defarge and Dr Manette? Why is he in such a pitiful state?

Coursework done under controlled conditions as described above will usually be undertaken towards the end of your course. Most teachers will give you ample time to practise the necessary techniques before you are asked to undertake the real thing.

Possible assignments for selected texts

Wuthering Heights Emily Brontë

1 Write the diary Heathcliff might have kept describing some of the unhappy times he experienced in his younger years. You should put forward reasons explaining how his unhappy childhood and youth might have affected him in later life.

2 Cathy says she loves Edgar and also that she loves Heathcliff. If you were Cathy which one would you have married? Give your reasons.

3 After Cathy told Nelly that she was going to marry Edgar, Heathcliff disappeared for a long time. Write an account of his career during this time.

4 Within twenty-four hours of marrying Heathcliff, Isabella's love has turned to hatred. Write the secret diary Isabella might have kept explaining what life was like for her. In this diary she might also suggest why she thinks Heathcliff married her.

5 Write an article for your local newspaper describing reports from local people that the ghostly apparitions of Cathy and Heathcliff had been seen on the moors.

Notes

Refer to last chapter of novel in particular – Nelly's statement that the country folk would swear on the Bible that he *walks* – interview two different local people – interview Nelly and or Hareton if possible – refer to sightings – church, moor, even within the house – the old man by the kitchen fire – 'he has seen two on 'em' . . . chamber window . . . every rainy night – then report boy with sheep – boy crying – 'under t'nab' – his fear – dare not go past them – or sheep either – Nelly's fear of dark – is it all just rumour? (See final paragraph of novel. Include headlines etc if possible.)

Cider With Rosie **Laurie Lee**

1 Read the chapter entitled *First Light*. Write about moving house from the point of view of a child and then from the point of view of an adult.

2 As the two old Browns lie in their separate beds in the workhouse they reflect on their lives together. Write down their thoughts.

3 Write one of Uncle Sid's suicide notes explaining why he was going to kill himself 'this time'.

4 Read the chapter *Last Days* and describe the picnic from mother's point of view. How do you think she felt about the various disasters and everyone's behaviour? Do you think she might have thought of herself as a failure?

5 From what you have read about the courtship of his three sisters, do you think they married and settled down in the village? Where do you think they may have lived instead?

6 Write a full account of Laurie's mother.

Notes

Refer particularly to Chapter 7 and passingly to other sections of the book – her childhood – intelligence – dreaminess – left school early (at 13) – responsibility thrust on her by mother's illness – coping with her brothers – experience of domestic service in large houses – reminiscences of same – helps father in pub – housekeeper to widower – married him (though he already had 5 children) – later deserted – sentimental about her married life – own housekeeping chaotic – loved doing competitions in newspapers – unpredictable at times – unpunctual – a hoarder – collector of old china – wrote acidly about local characters – loved flowers – played piano – increasingly eccentric with age – died not long after death of her husband. Conclusion might stress genuineness, love of life, stamina, some creative ability (inherited by Laurie), individuality, influence.

The Day of the Triffids **John Wyndham**

1 Pretend you are Bill Mason on the day after 'the comet' has struck nearly everyone blind. Describe your feelings and how you tried to help people.

2 If you were the leader of a community of eight sighted men and fifteen blind ones, describe how you would organize life during your first week.

3 Describe in detail what it would be like to make a one-hundred mile journey by car three months after the comet had struck. Include references to the novel.

4 Was the catastrophe described in this novel caused by man or was it natural? Refer in detail to the text.

To Kill a Mockingbird Harper Lee

1 Write the kind of report Miss Caroline would have made on Scout, Walter Cunningham, Little Chuck Little and Burris Ewell.

2 Write an obituary in the *Maycomb Tribune* for Mrs Dubose.

3 Imagine you are Atticus defending Tom Robinson. Write your notes for the trial setting out how you intend to defend him.

Animal Farm George Orwell

1 Pretend you are Napoleon. Write notes on how you intend to take over from Farmer Jones as the ruler of Animal Farm and how you intend to safeguard your power (refer to incidents in the novel).

2 The author of this book describes it as 'a fairy story'. Do you think it is more than just a fairy story?

3 Describe how you see the farm developing over the next ten years.

4 Write some of Benjamin's memoirs as he looks back on the events of his life.

5 Write from Molly's point of view and explain why you had to leave the farm.

6 Writing from Napoleon's point of view say whether you are sorry or pleased when Boxer is taken away.

Fair Stood The Wind For France H. E. Bates

1 Write a diary from Francoise's point of view of the events which occur in the novel up until the time she and Franklin escape.

2 Francoise's father commits suicide. Write an obituary for him which will only be printed in the local newspaper after the liberation of France.

3 Read the events as they are related in Chapter 21. Writing from O'Connor's point of view say whether they have deepened your mistrust of the French.

4 Describe the events on the train from Francoise's standpoint. Try and recapture her feelings of suspense and fear as the train nears the frontier.

The Pearl John Steinbeck

1 Kino's manly pride spurs him on to resist the forces ranged against him. Make a list of these characteristics that mark him out as a man and relate these characteristics to events which occur later in the book.

2 As a policeman you have to conduct an investigation into the death of Coyatito and several unidentified bodies. Piece together some of the events as you may have heard them.

3 The novel ends on a sad note with Kino and Juana hurling the pearl back into the sea. Write a different, happy ending to the novel.

4 What do you think happened to Kino and Juana over the next twenty years? Base your answer on their characters and personalities as revealed in the story.

Of Mice And Men John Steinbeck

1 Write the letter which was found in Curley's wife's possessions giving her reasons for leaving him.

2 Write out an estate agent's hand-out for the farm Lennie and George would like to buy and the one they are working on.

3 Write a letter from Slim's point of view telling of recent events on the ranch. This letter should show something of your understanding of the events and the character.

4 Produce a seventh chapter for the novel, in which you describe what happens to George.

Notes

After the shooting George goes for that drink with Slim – they talk about the future – Slim understands – they plan to move on together – police however notified by Curley – George arrested – tried – compassion of judge – manslaughter (clever lawyer who argues he was protecting himself) – minimum prison term – others testify to George's character – Slim stands by him throughout – eventually joins Slim on a ranch after his release – make new life together – Slim marries – George continues to live with them – never forgets Lennie.

Shane Jack Schaefer

1 Imagine that you are young Bob Starrett. Write a letter to a friend describing how Shane arrived on your father's farm, how he settled down and what kind of man he was.

2 Joe says that life would lose its meaning if they ran away. Do you think he was right? Was his decision to stay justified by all the bloodshed it caused?

3 As the town sheriff you are asked to write a report on the death of Eddie Wright. Compile this report as objectively as you can.

4 Write an article for the newspaper either defending the rights of cattle ranchers *or* homesteaders.

5 Shane is a story which covers a great deal of violence. Do you think all of it is wrong, or that only some of it is? Give your reasons.

Buddy Nigel Hinton

1 As a policeman you are watching 56 Croxley Street. Write up your notes of what you discover during your surveillance.

2 Write a newspaper article describing the events leading up to Terry's arrest and court appearance. The article might start: Acting on the information received from a petty criminal's son . . . (Provide your own headline for this article.)

3 Tell the story of what becomes of Ralph.

4 Many years after the events described in *Buddy* he meets Charmian Rybeero. He tells her all the news of what has happened to him and his family since Terry has been released from prison. Write an account of what you think happened.

5 Write a letter to Buddy in which you offer him sound advice for the future.

Jane Eyre **Charlotte Brontë**

1 Writing as Jane, keep a diary which records your daily life at Lowood School.

2 Write a School Inspector's report of conditions at Lowood School, referring particularly to sanitation, food and the indoor temperature.

3 St John Rivers and Mr Rochester are both very different types of men, yet both have very positive qualities. Which one would you most like to have been? Give your reasons.

4 Write a report for your local newspaper describing the fire in which Mr Rochester received his injuries.

5 Write a script for the servant's gossip that might have resulted from the events surrounding Jane's intended marriage with Rochester.

6 Write a report for your local newspaper describing what happens during the wedding ceremony between Jane and Rochester.

7 Jane keeps a secret diary in which she records some of the strange happenings at Thornfield. Describe some of these frightening experiences as Jane would have seen them.

Lord of the Flies **William Golding**

1 One of the implications of *Lord of the Flies* is that if there were no adults about to keep order many boys would become savages. Write a reasoned answer, saying whether you agree or disagree with this.

2 Ralph and Jack are friends at first, but they are very different. Ralph looks forward to the time when they will be rescued but Jack appears to be interested only in hunting. Which one of the boys would you have followed? Give your reasons.

3 Ralph cried with emotion when he knew that they were going to be saved. Was this because he was ashamed in some way or was it because he was relieved at being saved from a horrible death? Writing as Ralph explain your emotions at this time, referring back to events in the novel which may be responsible for your current state.

5 Of the five main characters in the book: Ralph, Jack, Roger, Simon and Piggy, which one would you most like to have been and which one would you least like to have been? Find as many reasons as you can.

Across the Barricades Joan Lingard

1 The British soldiers in Belfast had a difficult job. They had to keep their tempers whilst all around were losing theirs. Writing as one of the soldiers, describe your feelings in this divided city.

2 In Chapter 15 Kevin is wrongly accused of possessing a gun. Write the statement he would have made to the police.

3 In Belfast the police will keep files on anyone they suspect of terrorist activities. Taking some of the central characters in the novel, write up some of these files.

4 Sadie keeps a diary of the events in Belfast which concern her and Kevin. Write up some of these entries.

5 Writing as a journalist working for a newspaper that speaks for the Catholic community, describe the army's search of Kevin's and his neighbours' houses.

6 Sadie writes to her parents explaining why she has left with Kevin. Write this letter.

7 Write a final chapter for the book describing what happens to the couple in England.

1984 George Orwell

1 Write a personal description for your grandchildren of what life is like in Airstrip one, the third most populous province of Oceania.

2 Compile two or three pages of a prole newspaper for the April day in 1984 on which the story begins, keeping to events either mentioned or likely to have occurred then.

3 Mrs Parsons's two children belong to the spies, the Party's juvenile organization. Write the script for an imaginary denunciation they might make of a neighbour's family.

4 Write Winston's confession after he has undergone interrogation, making sure that you bring Julia into it.

5 O'Brien reveals that he has been watching Winston for seven years. Imagine that O'Brien has kept a secret diary right up until the time of Winston's release from the *Ministry of Love*. Write a selection of entries that he might have made.

6 Writing from Winston's point of view describe his feelings on hearing the victory announcement on the telescreen at the Chestnut Tree Cafe.

A Kestrel for a Knave Barry Hines

1 Mr Farthing has been asked to write a detailed report on Billy Casper's attitude to school. Compile this report.

2 Writing as if you were Billy, describe how you have trained Kes.

3 Mr Gryce, the headmaster, has been asked to write an article for the local newspaper about his views on the significant changes which have occurred in education over the past fifteen years. Write this article.

4 Jud explains to one of his women friends why he has killed Billy's hawk. Give an account of this explanation.

Z for Zachariah R. C. O'Brien

1 Write a medical report on the symptoms of radiation sickness as they affect John Loomis.

2 Writing from the point of view of Loomis give an account of his memories of Anne after she has left the valley.

3 Anne has been asked to prepare a survival manual based on her experiences. Compile this manual after carefully selecting your information from the book.

High Wind in Jamaica **Richard Hughes**

1 Write an account of the earthquake for your local newspaper.

2 If you were offered the chance of sailing aboard the pirate ship Clorinda, or on any other ship, which would you choose and why?

3 Twenty years after these events Margaret writes an account of her experiences at the hands of the pirates. Write this account as seen through her eyes.

4 Writing from the point of view of Captain Johnson describe your feelings towards the children after the trial.

Far From the Madding Crowd **Thomas Hardy**

1 As a journalist you are asked to write an article for the *Wessex Times* about the fire at Bathsheba Everdene's farm. Write this article, bringing out clearly the part played by Gabriel Oak.

2 Write a dialogue (with dialect if possible!) of gossip at the Buck's Head concerning the death of Fanny Robin, bringing in the local characters who play some part in the novel.

3 Write an account of Troy's career from the time of his assumed drowning to his appearance at the Christmas party.

4 Boldwood's crime is represented as being the result of madness and his sentence is commuted to life imprisonment. Carefully compose the kind of appeal which would have been made on Boldwood's behalf to the Sheriff of Dorset and the Home Office.

Notes

Boldwood – age – general character – help given to others during his life – concern over Fanny Robin – local farmer – much respected – testimony of Gabriel about him included in the appeal – reserved – distant – efficient until overturned by feelings for Bathsheba – the valentine which changed his life – various episodes – the arrival of Troy – Troy's subsequent insults – his lonely walks at night – neglect of farm – conversations with Gabriel – meetings with Bathsheba – her reluctant promise – his obsession and fantasy (later revealed) of Bathsheba Boldwood – the party – final return of Troy – his actions – his touching of Bathsheba – the shooting. The appeal would stress *stability* of character before meeting Bathsheba, and *instability* since. As indicated above, use the text which underlines the general decency of the man before the terrible changes which have been wrought in him by his obsessions.

Great Expectations Charles Dickens

1 From the convict Magwitch's point of view describe your first meeting with Pip.

2 Write the letter Magwitch would have sent to Mr Jaggers informing him that he wanted Pip educated and brought up to be a person of 'great expectations'.

3 As a newspaper reporter write an article about the drowning of Compeyson and the rescue of Magwitch from the Thames. (Details of their past as revealed in the novel should be included.)

4 Describe Pip from the point of view of (a) Biddy (b) Jaggers (c) Pumblechook (d) Estella, at different times during the story.

5 In old age Pip writes a letter to a younger friend advising him about what he thinks makes a real gentleman. Write this letter.

Notes

Pip's recollections of childhood – Joe, Mrs Joe, Biddy, Miss Havisham, Estella – encounter with Magwitch – incidents and events – translation to London – abandons Joe – learns by life experience – misfortune – Magwitch his benefactor THEN realizes being a real gentleman consists of being sympathetic – genuine – kind – sincere – not snobbish – respecting people for what they are not what they seem – having genuine humility – moral standards – etc. Continue wherever possible to refer to the book and incidents in it which helped to show you what makes a gentleman consisted of. Add in any other points which seem appropriate.

Examples drawn from short stories

The Case For The Defence Graham Greene

1 Write a very sensational account of the trial for a tabloid newspaper.

2 Writing from Mrs Salmon's point of view describe your feelings as the accused are set free.

The Garbage Collector Ray Bradbury

1 Have you ever looked forward to doing something and then found it was a great disappointment? Write about it.

2 Write a story about a man who is very happy in his work until something happens which makes him want to give it up.

A Sound of Thunder Ray Bradbury

1 Write the advertising handout for the Adventure Holidays, Time Safari, Inc.

2 Write a sensational account of Eckel's death for a tabloid newspaper under the heading *HORROR SLAYING*.

The Bike Alan Sillitoe

1 If you were Colin explain why you would not tell the truth about the bike?

2 What do you think of Colin? Is he a fool? Is he really as big a criminal as Bernard?

The Verger Somerset Maugham

1 What would you have done if you had been made redundant like the verger?

2 If you were the vicar of the church where the verger was employed, explain why you felt it necessary to replace him.

Late Night on Watling Street Bill Naughton

1 You enter a typical transport café after you have made a long journey up Watling Street. What are your emotions and feelings? (What do you think it is like to be a transport driver?)

2 When the police arrived at the scene of this horrific crash they would have had to make a report of what they had seen. Write this report, starting with the words: 'At 10:30pm on Friday, January 15th, I was driving . . .'

Example from non-fiction

My Family and Other Animals Gerald Durrell

1 There are many funny episodes and observations in *My Family and Other Animals*. By referring to the text, bring out the qualities of humour which you find most attractive.

2 Write about the island of Corfu as it is described and revealed in the book.

3 From Gerald Durrell's accounts, many of the animals appear to have human characteristics. Give examples from any *three* of the animals to indicate their feelings and reactions in given situations.

4 Compare and contrast any two animals of the same species in some detail.

5 Write about your favourite animals in the book, bringing out Durrell's powers of description and his detail in your account.

6 Write about any animal you have either (a) raised or (b) bought/acquired, over a period of time. Try to be as precise and as descriptive as Durrell is in order to capture your reader's interest.

Notes

Example used here – a pony – when acquired – where – brief details – birth – age – colouring – type – any particular characteristics – temperament – daily routine – grooming – feeding – general health attention – exercise – detailed description – choose words carefully in description – make it come alive for reader – time you spend with pony – does he/she get on with others? – where stabled – riding – classes – events. This brief outline is for one particular type of animal. You should draw up draft outline for a much-loved pet. Remember that your words must bring out the main characteristics of the animal and your reasons for liking it.

Conclusion

It may be that none of the texts mentioned in this book have been read by you. They are not on your list, your teacher has guided you towards others and these form the main part of your study. Bearing in mind what you have read here, make up your own assignments from the kind of questions and assignments we have given. This should not be difficult since, as we have indicated earlier, fiction almost always has (a) characters; (b) a theme or themes; (c) a setting or a variety of settings; (d) a plot, and often sub-plots; (e) the use of dialogue; (f) the use of descriptive or figurative language (that is, the use of metaphors, similes, personification, for example).

There are a number of other things you might consider. Is the writing modern, contemporary, or is it definitely set in the past? If you can identify the time, do so; there may be historical and social references, as with a novelist like Dickens. In *Oliver Twist* Dickens is attacking the Poor Law, the treatment of the inmates of workhouses on Parish relief. In *A Tale of Two Cities* Dickens is writing a graphic story which describes events before the French Revolution and during its most extreme excesses, with a marked emphasis on the horrific rule of the guillotine. As we have seen with *To Kill a Mockingbird*, the background of the local historical time – 1933–35 – is important for two reasons. Firstly, the prejudices of the American Civil War, which was fought largely on the issue of slavery, are still very much alive in the town of Maycomb. Secondly, the thirties sees the emergence of the virulent Nazism in Germany under Hitler which leads to the Second World War. This wider background serves to highlight the events in Maycomb. It is a mirror-image of contemporary evil.

We have indicated the importance of background to the development or conditioning of character. Let us consider again *To Kill a Mockingbird* as this novel possesses so many of the qualities of literature which you will be studying. Firstly, it has the intimacy of the (supposedly) autobiographical narrator Scout. This gives the novel a sharpness of narrative focus, and you must remember as you study it that everything is seen through the eyes of Scout. Not only does this give a graphic immediacy to the narrative, it also limits what is seen, it leaves mysteries unresolved and it entails guesswork on the reader's part. We also have to remember that what Scout tells us is informed with hindsight – behind the little girl we see the grown-up narrator. In a good novel we believe in the world which we as readers are being invited to enter. It does not matter if that world is set in the past, the present or the future, or in a different geographical or time location to our own. It is how the writer creates that world, how he or she peoples it, which absorbs our attention and our imagination. In *To Kill a Mockingbird* Scout has a number of experiences which condition her, which help to make her what she is and what she becomes.

We have concentrated, perhaps, on the racial element and the anti-humanitarian element to the exclusion of others. There is, for example, the superb narrative tension and excitement and, initially, mystery, of Chapter 28. Jem and Scout are followed home after the pageant and, such is the skill of the writer, that we are inclined to think it may well be Cecil Jacobs who is trying to scare them. But it is much more serious than that. Scout is attacked, through her blurred vision we know that someone has attacked her attacker, and she also sees Jem being carried towards the house. The tension is maintained when she manages to free herself from the chicken wire with the help of her aunt, worries about Jem, sees a stranger in the house and learns from the sheriff Heck Tate that Bob Ewell is dead under a tree outside. He has been stabbed. Now note that we have kept here to the revelations and action of just one chapter. In fact the secret of who the man in the room is is cunningly held back, so that the chapter ends on a note of expectation. Readers of this book will note one very important thing which cannot be fully illustrated in our summary above, and that is that plot, character, setting, theme, language are all involved. Consequently the scope for writing a passage of appreciation on this chapter alone would mean that you should be aware of the many points that we have made earlier if you are to do it full justice.

Read alertly as you study your texts, and note down points of character and style, of plot and setting, of language and theme, and you should be able to make your personal response to any text clear. When you are reading do not *waste time*. Give yourself to it with discipline and imagination. By all means read a novel or a story or a work of non-fiction at speed, enjoying it as you go, perhaps pausing occasionally to check a fact or a difficult word or phrase, or to make a brief note of something that you particularly like. When you have found out what it is about, go back and evaluate your reading by noting characteristics, of characters and of expression, and of the other aspects that we have mentioned above. Test your views in class discussion, and note class discussion and your teacher's views about the texts, making notes wherever possible and testing your own views against them later by looking again at the book. Literature is about exploration, what you find, what is revealed to you, what you experience as you are reading, what you experience as a result of your reading. Writing about literature is re-exploration, undertaken as a result of a close look at the works you are studying. It is also the beginning of imaginative development as you set down your thoughts and interpretations of what you have read. You will also learn to write imaginatively on your own account, thus developing your expression and personality and reaching levels of positive fulfilment.

Index to texts used

Titles published in the Brodie's Notes series

Henry Fielding Joseph Andrews Tom Jones

F. Scott Fitzgerald The Great Gatsby

E. M. Forster Howards End A Passage to India
Where Angels Fear to Tread

William Golding Lord of the Flies The Spire

Oliver Goldsmith She Stoops to Conquer

Graham Greene Brighton Rock The Power and the Glory
The Quiet American The Human Factor

Thom Gunn and Ted Hughes Selected Poems

Thomas Hardy Chosen Poems of Thomas Hardy
Far from the Madding Crowd Jude the Obscure
The Mayor of Casterbridge Return of the Native
Tess of the d'Urbervilles The Trumpet-Major The Woodlanders

L, P. Hartley The Go-Between The Shrimp and the Anemone

Joseph Heller Catch-22

Ernest Hemingway A Farewell to Arms For Whom the Bell Tolls
The Old Man and the Sea

Barry Hines A Kestrel for a Knave

Gerard Manley Hopkins Poetry and Prose of Gerard Manley Hopkins

Henry James Washington Square

Ben Jonson The Alchemist Volpone

James Joyce A Portrait of the Artist as a Young Man Dubliners

John Keats Selected Poems and Letters of John Keats

Ken Kesey One Flew over the Cuckoo's Nest

Rudyard Kipling Kim

D. H. Lawrence The Rainbow Selected Tales Sons and Lovers

Harper Lee To Kill a Mockingbird

Laurie Lee As I Walked out One Midsummer Morning
Cider with Rosie

Thomas Mann Death in Venice Tonio Kröger

Christopher Marlowe Doctor Faustus Edward the Second

W. Somerset Maugham Of Human Bondage

Gavin Maxwell Ring of Bright Water

Thomas Middleton The Changeling

Arthur Miller The Crucible Death of a Salesman

John Milton A Choice of Milton's Verse Comus and Samson
Agonistes Paradise Lost I, II

Sean O'Casey Juno and the Paycock
The Shadow of a Gunman and the Plough and the Stars

George Orwell Animal Farm 1984

John Osborne Luther

Alexander Pope Selected Poetry

J. B. Priestley An Inspector Calls

J. D. Salinger The Catcher in the Rye

Siegfried Sassoon Memoirs of a Fox-Hunting Man

Peter Shaffer The Royal Hunt of the Sun

William Shakespeare Antony and Cleopatra As You Like It
Coriolanus Hamlet Henry IV (Part I) Henry IV (Part II)
Henry V Julis Caesar King Lear Love's Labour's Lost
Macbeth Measure for Measure The Merchant of Venice
A Midsummer Night's Dream Much Ado about Nothing
Othello Richard II Richard III Romeo and Juliet The Sonnets
The Taming of the Shrew The Tempest Twelfth Night
The Winter's Tale

G. B. Shaw Androcles and the Lion Arms and the Man
Caesar and Cleopatra The Doctor's Dilemma Pygmalion Saint Joan

Richard Sheridan Plays of Sheridan: The Rivals; The Critic;
The School for Scandal

John Steinbeck The Grapes of Wrath Of Mice and Men The Pearl

Tom Stoppard Rosencrantz and Guildenstern are Dead

J. M. Synge The Playboy of the Western World

Jonathan Swift Gulliver's Travels

Alfred Tennyson Selected Poetry

William Thackeray Vanity Fair

Flora Thompson Lark Rise to Candleford

Dylan Thomas Under Milk Wood

Anthony Trollope Barchester Towers